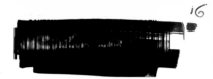

16

D1383154

DATE DUE

AUG 2 2 2016			
			PRINTED IN U.S.A.

THE BASIC
BELIEFS OF
JUDAISM

THE BASIC BELIEFS OF JUDAISM

A Twenty-first-Century Guide to a Timeless Tradition

Lawrence J. Epstein

JASON ARONSON

Lanham • Boulder • New York • Toronto • Plymouth, UK

Published by Jason Aronson
A wholly owned subsidiary of Rowman & Littlefield
4501 Forbes Boulevard, Suite 200, Lanham, Maryland 20706
www.rowman.com

10 Thornbury Road, Plymouth PL6 7PP, United Kingdom

British Library Cataloguing in Publication Information Available

Library of Congress Cataloging-in-Publication Data

Epstein, Lawrence J. (Lawrence Jeffrey)
  The basic beliefs of Judaism : a twenty-first-century guide to a timeless
tradition / Lawrence J. Epstein.
     pages cm
  Includes bibliographical references and index.
  ISBN 978-0-7657-0969-1 (cloth : alk. paper)—ISBN 978-0-7657-0970-7
(electronic) 1. Judaism. 2. Jewish way of life. I. Title.
  BM562.E67 2013
  296.3—dc23   2013015985

∞™ The paper used in this publication meets the minimum requirements
of American National Standard for Information Sciences—Permanence of
Paper for Printed Library Materials, ANSI/NISO Z39.48-1992.

Printed in the United States of America

For Sharon, of course

CONTENTS

ACKNOWLEDGMENTS

I sought advice for this book from people who had more knowledge than I did. They were shockingly abundant. Happily, they were also kind and generous with their time and their thoughts.

It is a ritual of politeness for authors to note that ultimately the responsibility for the contents and shape of the book rests on the writer. Such a statement is particularly important in this book because it is a strain of the imagination to believe that any of those who helped me accept all or many of the interpretations in the book. That they still helped says a lot about their character, including their intellectual tolerance and in many cases their friendship. Here are the particulars of my debt for help with the book.

Stewart Ain, a reporter at the *Jewish Week* in New York, who, both in his articles and in conversations, provided insights.

Rabbi Bob Alper, "the world's only practicing clergyman doing stand-up comedy . . . intentionally," sent me plenty of very funny jokes.

I thank Rabbi Benjamin Blech, author of such books as *The Complete Idiot's Guide to Understanding Judaism*, for his help and his moving message to me as I was recovering from a serious health problem.

Rabbi Celso Cukierkorn always is someone I can learn from regarding conversion to Judaism. I appreciate his constant support.

Bonny Fetterman, for reading the book as a work in progress.

Rabbi Adam Fisher, an author himself, and a longtime friend, listened, probed, and then made observations and suggestions that were crucial to the book's composition.

Rabbi Edward Friedman, for his reading suggestions about the issue of a Jewish mission.

Donna Halper, author and media historian, always provides materials and advice. I've relied on her suggestions for many books.

Rabbi David Kalb is the director of Jewish education for the Bronfman Center for Jewish Life at 92nd Street Y. He offered important perspectives and insights on the issues covered in the book.

Rabbi Stephen Karol of Temple Isaiah in Stony Brook, New York, is my rabbi. I've attended many of his classes and always learned from them.

Arthur Kurzweil is a gifted author, editor, lecturer, magician, genealogist, and student of Rabbi Adin Steinsaltz. Arthur has been my editor and a cherished friend for many decades. He provided important suggestions for the book.

Abe Novick, president of AbeBuzz, always has good ideas, perhaps because he is such a good writer.

For bibliographical advice, I turned, as I often do, to Kevin Proffitt, senior archivist for research and collections at the American Jewish Archives, who, as always, had excellent advice.

Rabbi Dr. Kerry M. Olitzky, author and executive director of the Jewish Outreach Institute, for suggesting some important reading.

Dr. Marla Segol, professor, The Institute of Jewish Thought and Culture, the University at Buffalo, for her support and suggestions.

I thank Rabbi Joseph Telushkin, author of *Jewish Literacy: The Most Important Things to Know about the Jewish Religion, Its People, and Its History* among many other books, for his kind words and help in adapting his account about how he came to embrace vegetarianism.

Diane Tobin, president of the Institute for Jewish and Community Research, for her suggestions.

Rabbi Joseph S. Topek, director of the Hillel Foundation for Jewish Life, Stony Brook University, made interesting observations about what subjects students were interested in learning about.

Stephen Weitzman, a member of the Union for Reform Judaism's North American Board, gave me important insights about subjects to cover in the book.

I thank Rabbi David Wolpe, author of such books as *Why Faith Matters*, for advice about including the story in this book about his father.

I'd also like to thank Marian Guralnick, Gladys Rothbell, Dr. Richard Tuckman, and Rabbi Harvey Witman for their suggestions.

The people at Jason Aronson were wonderful to work with from beginning to end. Lindsey Porambo has a keen editorial eye matched by a warm and supportive approach. That's a pretty good combination for an editor. Julie Kirsch, the publisher of Jason Aronson, was crucially vital in the book's inception and development. I'd like to thank everyone else at Jason Aronson for their first-class help as well as the three anonymous members of the Library Advisory Board for Aronson who evaluated the proposal.

Doug Rathgeb, a friend for fifty years, always listens and, as a writer himself, always has helpful advice.

My great friend Assemblyman Mike Fitzpatrick provided invaluable help along the way. What would I do without him?

Don Gastwirth, my literary agent, is always there. His brother, Dr. Joseph Gastwirth, is a constant source of well-wishes and support.

My cousins Toby Everett and Dr. Sheldon Scheinert are closer than cousins. They have always provided a supply of pleasure and strength for me.

My brother, Richard, always receives a call from me when I get an idea for a book. I won't proceed without his advice and help. His wife, Perla, and their children and grandchildren are wonderful in their help.

My late parents, Fred and Lillian Epstein, of blessed memory, showed me how to lead a moral life. All my work is in their honor.

My love and admiration for my children is unbounded. Michael and his wife, Sophia Cacciola; Elana Reiser and her husband, Justin; Rachel Eddey and her husband, John; and Lisa Christen and her husband, Florian, all are beyond generous in their devotion, time, intelligence, and kindness. Each has helped me with this book. I also thank all my in-laws and other relatives who are part of the family life.

My grandchildren are the special lights in my life.

My wife, Sharon, is irreplaceable in her encouragement, her companionship, and her love. She's the one who has had to provide help during a difficult time in my life and had to listen to what must have seemed like my endless mutterings, concerns, and expressions of joy about the career of this book.

PREFACE

I was sitting in a crowded college classroom. Everyone was listening to the Holocaust survivor describe living through hell. He had been imprisoned in several concentration camps where, among his jobs, he had to remove dead bodies. He had been on a death march. In a calm voice, he described his life in the camps and how his knowledge of several languages had helped him live. When the speaker finished, he asked if there were any questions. Everyone in the audience was stunned. No one could move, much less frame a question.

I was one of the two professors who taught the class. I didn't know what to do. The survivor seemed eager for questions. It was my job to ask one. A single question pulsated through my brain. I didn't know whether or not to ask it. The silence continued, and I had to act. I nervously raised my hand. He nodded at me, and I said I was so overwhelmed by the talk that I was left with one haunting question that I normally would be too embarrassed to ask but couldn't stop myself. The survivor waited patiently.

I said to him, "After all you've been through, do you believe in God?"

The survivor hesitated for a moment. I thought he was angry at me for the question. But he continued in a soft voice. He said that to answer the question he had to tell the class a story.

After the war, he had married another survivor, a woman who had been subjected to experimentation. He didn't have to describe the nature of the experiments. We all understood. The result, he said, was that despite the couple's efforts they could have no children.

After the Israeli victory in the Six-Day War of 1967, the couple traveled to Jerusalem to pray at the Western Wall, which was in Jewish control for the first time in almost two thousand years. The wife was tired when they arrived in Jerusalem late at night, but she encouraged her husband to go immediately to the Wall. The survivor got to the Wall and began to cry. He could not pray because of his anger at God.

Suddenly a young religious student appeared. The survivor was shocked because the student looked just as the survivor had at that age. The student approached the survivor, reminding him of the ancient tradition of putting a note in the cracks of the Wall. The survivor was reluctant, but the student kept encouraging him until the survivor took a scrap of paper and wrote "I want a baby" in Hebrew. He tearfully stuck the paper into the Wall.

The survivor then prayed and looked around to thank the student, but the young man was gone.

The survivor again paused in his story and looked at the class. There was complete silence for a few seconds. He then told us that ten months after his visit to the Wall he and his wife had a baby girl.

So, he asked, how could he say for sure even after all he'd been through that there is no God? All he knew is that if he ever encountered God, he had a lot of questions.

The survivor's story has accompanied me during the ensuing years as I pondered, read, learned from others, and taught
about God, Judaism, and how we deal with the most profound
questions of human existence. I knew there were a variety of
religious reactions by Holocaust survivors. Some didn't believe
in God. Some were so angry at God they could no longer pray.
Some didn't even want to be Jewish any longer.

I understood the range of reactions, but I was particularly
struck by people with the undeniable urge to continue as Jews.
This led me to wonder why Judaism is so powerful, so filled with
meaning that the most devastating acts of evil cannot crush the
spark of Judaism within those who suffered. This book is an attempt to answer that question.

When I first considered writing this book, I pictured people
I had met. Some were just curious about Judaism. Some were
romantically attached to a Jewish partner and were considering
becoming Jewish themselves. Some had unpleasant memories
of childhood Jewish educations or services at which they felt
ignorant or uncomfortable. These memories had led them to
neglect learning about Judaism. These people I knew were curious about Judaism's basic beliefs. I wanted to invite them to
learn about how Judaism interprets the world.

I also knew many intelligent people who thought about and, at
times, struggled with all the nagging, painful, exhilarating, wondrous questions of why we are here and what we're supposed to do
with our lives. They were intellectually nimble, unfrightened, and
honest seekers, animated by ethical sensitivity and well informed
about a broad range of up-to-date knowledge. They wondered if
Judaism was compatible with modern science and whether they
could honorably believe in the Jewish faith today. Some thought
Judaism just a venerable collection of ancient myths more suitable to a museum than to our mobile devices. I wanted to invite
these people to explore their questions about Judaism.

For all these readers, I wanted to try to organize the beliefs of the Jewish faith in such a way that those interested could study it, learn what Judaism has to teach, and see for themselves what they concluded.

It is not the goal of the book to challenge anyone's faith (or faithlessness) or to change anyone's belief system. Rather I mean it as a guide for readers to learn about Judaism; to examine or reexamine the religious questions they have in their lives; and, in so doing, to ponder how they organize the ideas that guide their lives. I also mean the book as a challenge for all of us to examine the beliefs we cherish and live by or to explore what those beliefs are if we can't articulate them. Franz Kafka once wrote that "a book must be the ax for the frozen sea within us."

All readers of the book are asked to consider what lies in their own frozen sea. It was a Hasidic master who noted that all people must discover their own unique way in Judaism and then live by the light shed by that way, by the path it leads them along in life. They can be true to the Jewish religion most faithfully by being true to themselves.

A coherent theology, though, is not necessarily identical to leading a full spiritual life. Our lives are lived from within. It is an individual's psychological experience that often provides sufficiently convincing proof of whether God is present or not in the person's life. For many people, faith is more important than belief. They live by trust and hope, not by a religious ideology.

Still, while Judaism is more guided by the ethical than the speculative, being a spiritual being is insufficient as well. Genuine spiritual experiences need to be intellectually justifiable. And so I mean this book to be a blend of the intellectual and the personal.

My approach is to take the basic beliefs of Judaism and explain them, try to provide insights into how you might analyze them, and try to be respectful of all points of view. Analysis aims for subtlety and nuance. Ideology aims for simplicity. Issues of Jewish belief deserve analysis.

Such efforts are challenging. It is difficult to chart the logical geography of Jewish beliefs, the place of each individual one in relationship to all the others. Many beliefs could have been put in various places or overlap. Almost every belief discussed could have been expanded. The book is not meant to be a definitive guide but a gateway to the vast treasures of Jewish literature and the varied experiences of Jewish life. The goal of the book is, in part, to create interest in readers to explore other works and to become part of the Jewish community by joining and participating in Jewish institutions.

I also hope to get all of us to see our beliefs more explicitly, to recognize the presuppositions, the assumptions that we carry with us all the time and aren't always aware of it.

This book interprets Judaism as a belief system. The term *belief system* refers to a set of beliefs that an individual or community follows, such as about what is right and wrong and what is true and false. A belief is separate from a certainty. Belief requires a mental attitude of accepting a proposition or set of propositions without the certain knowledge that such a belief is true or can be justified. Sometimes *belief system* refers to a faith independent of the formal acceptance of a religion. In this book *belief system* is shorthand for a religious belief system based on facts but acknowledging the role of assertions beyond factual proof.

While Judaism is a belief system, it is a special kind of belief system, one that is flexible rather than rigid, one that gives choices within an extremely wide range rather than dictates required answers, one that does not see other people as compelled to accept it or be refused salvation, and a system that leads to moral action rather than being satisfied with beliefs alone. Indeed, as a special kind of belief system, Judaism is connected to and inseparable from obligations and activities. This connection is important, for without it, seeing Judaism as a belief system might imply that Judaism is just a religion, and as a religion, is just a belief system. This sort of reductionism, though, is inadequate to capture the crucial nature of moral action that stems from the belief system. Judaism cannot survive as just a series of intellectual beliefs. It requires observances by a community. A belief system can offer spiritual guidance to an individual, but Judaism includes joining together. A person needs to be religious rather than just spiritual because as a community people share human relationships. They can accomplish goals and actions that they couldn't accomplish on their own. They have in a community a deepened sense of purpose. The individual and communal goals of Judaism can be seen in the mitzvot and in the section on missions in chapter 6.

Why do religions have belief systems? Why are they valuable and needed? A complete religion is not limited to its prayers, holy days, and rituals. A religion must provide explanations about, for example, the nature and purposes of God and all the questions that stem from these explanations. Why, for example, do innocent children suffer deadly disease? A religion must offer its followers an ethical code, rules by which they can live. As Benjamin Disraeli, a British prime minister of Jewish origin, put it: "Duty cannot exist without faith." We cannot know how to act if we do not know what to believe.

As we examine our Jewish views, it is crucial to remember that there is not one single Jewish belief system to explain. Rather there is a range of such beliefs. Still, there are borderlines that define what makes a belief fall outside Judaism. There are historical examples. I will provide traditional and contemporary interpretations.

As the book's subtitle suggests, this book focuses on contemporary interpretations. I try, for example, to take natural and social science findings seriously, though I am not an expert in these fields. When appropriate, I try to see how Judaism can be interpreted in the light of contemporary science, to take its basic beliefs and connect them to contemporary knowledge.

It is also possible in discussing Judaism to talk of a "worldview." A "worldview" means a comprehensive system describing God, the natural world, and humanity. It includes how humans should live their lives and a theory about what happens after they die. It includes the beliefs and ideas an individual uses to interpret existence. The terms *belief system* and *worldview* are used instead of *theology* to indicate that the book is not just a theory of God and instead of *philosophy* to indicate that it is not just reliant on the rational methods used by philosophers and is not structured the way a philosophical argument would be.

This is a story with a very clear beginning. The story of the basic beliefs of Judaism starts with the most fascinating of possible characters, God. We start our search by considering the Being who, according to Jewish tradition at least, created the cosmos and human beings, who yearns for a moral partner and a people to teach about the moral rules of the road, the crucial tasks that humans are called upon to accomplish in life, the temptations flying all around them that they must ignore or overcome if they surrender to them. This God is a tough character to begin with because we can't ask God any questions. We can't see or hear God. There are no images, no pictures or sightings of God. How can we mere mortals possibly understand who this God is or what God wants of us?

After a discussion of God, the story continues in a chronological way. God first created the natural world (or it was created in another fashion) prior to the appearance of humans, and so the cosmos is the next subject, followed by humanity, and then the appearance of the Jewish people and their historic spiritual journey.

Finally, after the Jewish people, the next stage is the Jewish self, the individual in the world. After a consideration of the ethical foundations for a good life, the individual is considered as a marriage partner and family member and then a member of the wider community. The final consideration involves the Jewish beliefs about the death of each individual and the possibilities of the afterlife.

At each stage, readers will be encouraged to engage the material, to enter into a dialogue with it, in order to define their own Jewish worldview, not just from their own lives but also from the traditional sources of Jewish thought as well as contemporary knowledge. Constructing such a personal Jewish worldview that is grounded in a careful examination of Jewish sources is religiously empowering. Indeed, it can be empowering only because Judaism has no fixed dogma. The Jewish understanding of being in a partnership with God has its analogue of being in a partnership with tradition. Individuals are not religious robots. They have free will and probing minds. They can and are encouraged to lead an examined Jewish life.

After I provide a background and try to consider how to think about various Jewish beliefs including contemporary ones, I will offer suggestions about where readers can go to find a personal connection to Judaism. These spiritual suggestions are meant to prompt readers to think of their own sources for learning, ones that will lead to their own insights and provide questions both for individuals and for groups.

For example, I encourage readers to begin with a journal, to jot down their own ideas as they read, and then at the end of each chapter read over the notes. Some readers may even wish to write their own views in a more organized way. At the end, those who take this approach will have constructed their own Jewish belief system.

Precisely because Judaism is not a cold and calculated philosophical religion but a living faith, I have included true stories, quotations, and other materials that provide seasoning to the descriptive prose and provide a sense of not only what Jews believe but also how they feel as they believe.

The difficult goal of the book is to enable readers to formulate more precise questions about their Jewish beliefs and to expand the range and complexity of their often-tentative answers. I'm not sure how much I can contribute to this goal, but I hope working together with readers will provide insightful steps on the journey to the goal.

I recommend that the book be read in the order in which it was written, especially if you are interested in constructing your own belief system, because the material, to the best of my ability, is presented in an intellectually hierarchical fashion, with one section leading to the next. For those who wish to focus on discrete questions, it is certainly possible to read the chapter that deals with the question.

The book is meant for a wide variety of people, for adult Jews wishing to connect more fully or tentatively reconnect to their intellectual heritage, for students exploring the borderlines of the Jewish belief system, for Jewish spiritual leaders and educators, for Gentiles who wish to explore Judaism, and for anyone else interested in how to construct a belief system.

A note on language is necessary. For many centuries God was referred to as "He" in many texts, such as the Torah, prayer books, and other works, holy and otherwise. It is not a matter of political correctness but religious precision to note that God does not have a sexual identity, so using either "He" or "She" to describe God is inaccurate and misleading. Similarly, writers have used the masculine form to refer to all people. I have in my writing avoided language that erases the presence of women.

However, translating already-existing historical texts into an inclusive language is a matter of taste. Doing so is certainly understandable and well-meaning. I have tried to avoid such texts and other writing. But I have retained the masculine when it existed in texts or someone else's writing to reflect the original accurately. I invite readers who wish to translate from the masculine to more inclusive language to do so as they read.

And so, we begin what I hope will turn out to be an interesting and helpful journey.

❶

IN SEARCH OF THE
BASIC BELIEFS OF JUDAISM

There is a Jewish story about a young child in synagogue. The congregation is praying, but the child is unable to read Hebrew and so cannot participate. The child's mother suddenly realizes that her youngster is reciting the Hebrew alphabet over and over. The mother asks, "Why do you just keep repeating the Hebrew letters?" The child looks up and responds, "I figure that God can put the letters together in the right order."

Some of us who are Jewish feel like that when it comes to the basic beliefs of Judaism. We don't know the language. We're not even sure we know the alphabet. An alphabet has an order. It is comprehensive in that it includes every letter and through the letters every word. But how many of us can describe the Jewish articles of faith for ourselves or others in a complete, orderly way?

Part of the problem is that some of us have been taught that Judaism emphasizes action rather than beliefs. Everyone who is Jewish has either been born as a member of the Jewish people or converted to Judaism and is therefore part of the Jewish covenant, or agreement, with God. Such a membership in the

Jewish people has no required affirmation of a set of beliefs. Judaism has no body that can even impose such a dogma on Jews. For some Jewish thinkers, this fact means that Judaism is organic and not systematic, that it responds to the specific situations in which people find themselves in life rather than starting out with a set of beliefs and then applying those beliefs to situations as they arise. It should be noted that while there are no required beliefs, Judaism does have sacred texts and teachings. These are sometimes difficult to apply in everyday life, but the applications are what emerge from studying those texts and learning from rabbis and Jewish teachers.

We encounter the problem of what to believe all the time, sometimes in serious situations. Consider the choice Simon Wiesenthal described in his book *The Sunflower*. Wiesenthal, a Holocaust survivor who became a renowned Nazi hunter, relates an autobiographical incident in the book. As a prisoner in a labor detail near a hospital, Wiesenthal is brought to the bedside of a young German soldier who wants to confess his actions against Jews and be forgiven by a Jew before he dies. The book asks all readers to ponder the question of whether that forgiveness should be given. Such a decision requires readers to examine their deepest beliefs about the meaning of suffering and the possibilities of forgiveness. And the question arises: Do we decide on the basis of this individual dying soldier or do we start with a moral principle and apply it to the man? In real life, we probably would use both approaches, going from the specific situation of the soldier to a general rule about when forgiveness is justified or starting with the general rule and applying it to specific situations. Wiesenthal forms his conclusion, and there is a symposium of prominent people who also respond. For many of the Jewish responders, forgiveness is tied to repentance and restitution toward the person wronged.

If we observe our own potential reaction to the soldier in this dramatic example, it is helpful to our thinking to have some basic beliefs. It is not surprising, therefore, that many Jewish thinkers have concluded that it is too simplistic to consider Judaism a religion only of deed and not of creed. It is a religion of both, and they work together. Creed, a systematic statement of religious doctrines, is there to provide a meaning to our lives. But a creed is not enough. We need actions that stem from that creed to provide our life with purpose.

Another objection to the idea of having any religious belief system, including a Jewish one, is that religious language is either meaningless or hopelessly abstract. It's true that it is difficult to explain praying to an invisible God or seeking through prayer to praise that God or seek guidance. This linguistic difficulty does require anyone thinking about a Jewish belief system to be as precise as language allows in offering a definition of terms.

Beyond these, there is still another significant obstacle. Since Judaism does not offer an official set of beliefs, an official summary of the Jewish religion comparable, say, to a Catholic's catechism, it is notoriously difficult to define what exactly we mean by Judaism itself, as we'll see below.

There was once a famous and controversial rabbi who used an engaging rhetorical trick in debates. Suppose, for example, that the rabbi's debate opponent was named Kleinman. The rabbi would dismiss one of Kleinman's religious claims by stating, "That's not Judaism, that's Kleinmanism." In a sense, everyone who tries to offer an understanding of Judaism can be subjected to such a charge.

That is because every description of Jewish beliefs is an interpretation. Therefore, the discussion of Jewish beliefs in this book is not meant to be, and can't be, a definitive theory of Judaism. There is no such definitive theory. There are many doors that lead into the house of Judaism, many ways into an understanding of what it means to be Jewish.

The subtitle of this book calls it a "twenty-first-century guide." That is, while Jewish tradition is described, the book has a contemporary viewpoint. It is meant as a guide for those who wish to embrace Judaism using the latest knowledge available through the natural and social sciences and insights offered by the humanities. In such a guide there is less emphasis on traditional sources and more on modern sources. This change in emphasis leads to a different tone and sensibility, one perhaps more skeptical, more desirous of proof, more wary of the world. Sometimes the faddish masks what is eternally true, and so it is important to distinguish a contemporary fad or cultural reference from a useful contemporary outlook that adds insight to tradition. For example, seeing the often-overlooked role of women is crucial, as is reexamining beliefs considering that role, as is noting the contributions of converts to Judaism, including African Americans and others from non-traditional conversionary groups.

And what are "basic" beliefs? The basic beliefs refer to the ones that support all the others, the foundational, fundamental, underlying beliefs that allow other beliefs to be built on them. "Basic" also has the connotation of being elementary. That is true of this book in the sense that the book is aimed at the general reader, not the expert, and assumes no prior knowledge of Judaism or the Jewish faith.

It is important to try to be precise in definition and in stating the beliefs because there are great divides within Judaism, making it ever more difficult to define that faith. There are institutional differences among, for example, the groups termed *Orthodox*, *Conservative*, and *Reform*, among others. These movements have different emphases, different approaches to Jewish law, different prayer books and rabbinic seminaries. It is an oversimplification, but it is possible to consider the root difference among Jews to be between "strictly traditional" and "strictly modern" Jews. Of course, both Jews blend tradition and modernity to some extent, but, at the risk of simplification, stating starker differences can offer clarification to the views.

The five million American Jews belong to a variety of movements. Adherents of Orthodoxy generally believe that Jews should observe all the 613 mitzvot, or religious laws, enumerated in the Torah, most simply understood as the first five books of the Hebrew Bible. These laws include, for example, eating only kosher food; observing the rules of the Sabbath, such as refraining from work; and so on. The Orthodox believe that Jews are bound by religious law (the Halakhah). The Orthodox are themselves divided into various groups, such as modern Orthodox, who seek to integrate their faith and their lives with contemporary American society; the Hasidim, who tend to live separately in their own communities, have a distinctive form of dressing, and to varied extents shun the distractions of modernity; and what might be called the Yeshiva Jews, who were trained with a traditional Jewish education and are somewhere between the modern Orthodox and Hasidic worlds. All Orthodox Jews believe that God gave Moses the Torah, the written Torah and the oral Torah—the laws not written down on Mount Sinai but passed on verbally until they were written down in the Talmud.

In contrast to Orthodox Jews, followers of Reform Judaism, the largest of the Jewish movements in the United States, do not believe contemporary Jews are bound by the Halakhah; rather, they believe that it can influence but not rule behavior. Generally, Reform Jews believe in the individual autonomy of members of their faith, relying on a person's study and ethical sensitivity to provide a moral compass. Reform Judaism in recent years has become more observant, more interested in finding value in rituals and traditions. Reform Jews believe the Bible was a human product, though perhaps inspired by God. Reform Jews emphasize the prophetic tradition, especially its emphasis on helping those who are poor, hungry, and needy.

Followers of Conservative Judaism believe the Halakhah is binding upon its followers but emphasize its ability to evolve along with the perceptions and needs of the Jewish people. Conservative Jews are generally considered as religiously midway between the more traditional Orthodox and the more modern Reform.

Reconstructionist Judaism began out of a belief that there is not a supernatural God, that Judaism is a civilization, and that Jewish cultural experiences are the genuine reflections of religious life.

There are, additionally, large numbers of American Jews who do not belong, either formally or even intellectually, to any of these movements. Some practice Judaism on their own and are "just Jewish." Some are alienated from religious life but not from their Jewish identity. Some do not even think of themselves as Jewish. And there are other movements, such as Humanistic Judaism, whose followers assert that there is no supernatural God. Additionally, there are various emphases in Jewish life that can't really be called movements. Jewish Renewal, for example, wants to rekindle American Jews with a spirituality that has its origins in Hasidic or mystical experiences. Those drawn to Jewish Renewal characteristically meditate and employ music. Some focus on feminism or other progressive movements in Jewish life.

More generally, someone with a "traditional" view believes that some sacred Jewish literature contains the unchangeable words of God, that the 613 commandments express the will of God and therefore must be followed, and that modernity has too often betrayed and unfairly challenged the Jewish tradition and has resulted in the straying of many Jews from their ancestral faith.

Someone with a "modern" view, which is used in this book, in general incorporates the ideas and methodologies of the natural and social sciences. "Modern" Judaism welcomes political, social, and cultural integration of Jews within wider societies but specifically also within a Jewish belief system, a distinctive Jewish peoplehood, and a Jewish family and community. "Modern" Judaism takes the Bible seriously but not literally and applies scientific and literary methods to investigate the Bible and its text. In a classic formulation, modernity offers tradition a vote but not a veto over how to live a Jewish life.

Some beliefs change over time. The Talmud, for example, includes the poetic observation that "every blade of grass has its angel that bends over it and whispers 'Grow, grow.'" A modern Jew would not use such poetry but would employ a far less poetic but more scientific biological explanation of how grass grows.

Judaism is not even always defined as a religion, because such a definition centers on the idea that the faith follows a set of beliefs. Therefore, some define Judaism as a nation, a culture, an ethnicity, a people, a philosophy, a way of life—or, in Rabbi Mordecai Kaplan's insightful word, a civilization (which he later modified to "an evolving religious civilization").

The early Israelites did not have a concept of either Judaism or religion. They used the term *Torah* to mean their practices and their beliefs. The Hebrew word for Judaism, *yahadut*, first appeared in the Middle Ages. It is crucial to note that the word did not refer to what we now call religion, but included the idea of peoplehood (Jewry) and identity (Jewishness). These, along with the religious understanding of Judaism, were included in the word *yahadut*.

Judaism, then, was not strictly a religion prior to modern times because religion was not a separate strand of Jewish life but was interwoven with an entire communal existence that included culture and, often, legal autonomy.

The modern idea of religion as a segment of Jewish identity that focused, for example, on prayers and rituals developed as a response to the rise of the modern European nation-state and the emergence of Protestantism. Building on the thought of Moses Mendelssohn, modern Jews increasingly understood Judaism as a private and voluntary act. This was in sharp contrast to the Halakhic notion of Judaism as compulsory and mostly public. In this way, Jews presented themselves as similar to Protestants and loyal citizens to the emerging nations by accepting that the nations had sovereignty over them. This seemed like a good bargain, this reduction of Judaism to a religion. But the bargain led Jews to have a sometimes naive and dangerous faith both in the nation-states where they lived and in modernity itself.

Therefore, calling Judaism a religion is fraught with unexpected traps, but there isn't another English word that captures the borderlines of a belief system, so *religion* is used in this book. As mentioned in the preface, the conception here is that Judaism is a special kind of belief system, but it is now clear that in understanding what is included in the Jewish belief system, we have to go beyond a doctrinal list. We have to understand it as a "belief system" that includes the entire Jewish way of life, and that calling it a "religion" is a shorthand way to describe Judaism and is also misleading, for true Judaism is much more comprehensive than the word *religion* implies.

Any religion starts with the apprehension that there is a sacred reality apart from the natural reality of everyday life. Once this realization is achieved, adherents of a religion reorient their lives toward that sacred reality because the experiences of ordinary life pale in comparison to the experiences of the sacred life. This view implies that it is the sacred experiences that provide us with purpose and meaning and values. Religious people seek ways to connect themselves and their community to the sacred reality and to preserve those connections. Judaism, on this understanding, expresses the central truths about God, the world, and humanity. It offers the crucial insights we need to understand our place in the cosmos and the sort of lives we should lead. Judaism introduced the world to its understanding of that sacred reality as a single, unified Being, now often named God. The Jewish view emerged as one in which God expressed a moral will for humans to be good and appointed Jews to teach that moral lesson to the world. Jews, in turn, proved sometimes able and willing to act on God's will and sometimes not. Judaism expressed its beliefs through its conception of God, the revelation that God made, and the expression of that divine will, as well as a sense of peoplehood and interdependence of history and fate in an attempt to act together to meet God's will because collective action could accomplish more good than individual action.

Sometimes the word *religion* is contrasted with *spirituality*. The terms have traditionally been virtually synonymous, but for some, spirituality has come to mean a private, personal communion with a higher force without necessarily subscribing to the views of a particular religion or belonging to any religious community. As has been suggested, Judaism without its institutionally required set of beliefs has spirituality in this sense of the word built into it. Of course, Judaism, as opposed to the exclusively individual aspects of any understanding of spirituality, explicitly includes participating in a community. The point of the community is that individual efforts to understand the Divine need to be challenged, probed, questioned, and defended, and this can best be done in concert with other sincere believers who are attached to other understandings and can offer and receive guidance about the most important questions of the spiritual life. Being part of a group, that is, enhances individual spirituality rather than diminishes it.

Additionally, sometimes religion is understood as implying spiritual certainty, as though there is no room for doubt and no tolerance for it. It is telling that the Talmud opens with a question. That is symbolic of how Judaism proceeds. Questions are followed by discussions and different opinions. Certainty is characteristically a stranger.

Judaism encourages doubt in several ways, most principally by not having a fixed belief system. But the very word *Israel*, which in this case refers not to the nation but to the Jewish people, means those who wrestle with God, not those who believe in God. This literal wrestling took place when Jacob wrestled with an angel in the Bible. The tolerance for unbelief is widespread. There is, for example, the story of the Baal Shem Tov Israel ben Eliezer, who was the leader of Hasidism in Eastern Europe in the first half of the eighteenth century. According to the story, one day a man came to complain to the great Jewish sage. "My son has abandoned God," the sad man complained. "What shall I do?" The Baal Shem Tov looked at the man and said, "Love him more than ever." That is the Jewish attitude toward doubt. Here is a great Jewish teacher suggesting that a doubter not only not be pushed away but also be embraced ever tighter.

Despite Judaism's elusive definition, there have been many attempts to offer a systematic list of Judaism's basic ideas that underlie its practices and institutions. Additionally, many Jewish theologians and philosophers have examined the various ideas that make up Jewish doctrines.

The Mishnah (definitions of sacred texts can be found in the glossary), for example, in Sanhedrin 10:1 suggests that a portion in the World to Come will be denied to those who do not believe in the resurrection of the dead or the divine origin of the Torah, that is, God's revelation to people. Also banned will be Epicureans, followers of Epicurus, the Greek philosopher who was a materialist and who attacked the notion of a supernatural God affecting human life. Epicureans stood as a metaphor for all those who denied a supreme being.

The most famous list of the principles of the Jewish faith was written by Moses Maimonides (Moshe ben Maimon, or the Rambam, an acronym in Hebrew for the word *rabbi* and his name) in the twelfth century. Maimonides was the preeminent Torah scholar and philosopher of his era and is regarded as one of the most brilliant sages in all Jewish history. Nevertheless, despite all his learning and his sterling reputation, even Maimonides's principles are not regarded as binding. Here is a list, freely translated from Maimonides's Arabic writing, of his thirteen principles:

1. God created the cosmos.
2. God is one unified Being.
3. God does not have a physical body and cannot therefore be represented in bodily form or image.
4. God is an eternal Being, a Divine power who was there at the beginning of creation and will be present at its conclusion.
5. God is the only power worthy of our prayers.
6. God offered a revelation to prophets.
7. Moses is the greatest of all the prophets.
8. The Torah, God's revelation, was given directly to Moses.
9. The Torah contains eternal truth. It cannot be altered and cannot be replaced by another revelation.
10. God has foreknowledge of the future and knows the thoughts and actions of human beings.
11. God rewards those who obey his commandments and punishes those who disobey Divine laws.

12. God will one day send a Messiah to bring about a re-
    deemed world.
13. God will revive those who have died.

In part, Maimonides and other Jewish religious thinkers felt
obliged to create a clear statement of faith to defend Judaism
against heretical views. That's important because the act of such
self-defense is a useful reminder that a list of Jewish beliefs,
even if not authoritative, even if extraordinarily flexible in individual interpretation, nonetheless does have borders beyond
which followers cannot pass and remain religiously Jewish. In
the Rambam's case, for example, several of his principles were
specifically meant to challenge Christianity and Islam. In particular, the third principle was meant to challenge the Christian
view that God took bodily form. The sixth principle was meant
to confront the then-widespread claim that Mohammed was the
greatest prophet of God.

Maimonides's principles became enormously influential.
Even now, they are heard in summary form in Yigdal (meaning "Magnify"), a popular hymn sung in synagogues all over the
world as part of the opening of the morning service and also as
part of the close of the evening service.

There were many other formulations of a Jewish belief system. Just as an example, Hasdai Crescas, a medieval Jewish
philosopher who lived after Maimonides, believed in six principles that must be accepted: (1) God is omniscient; (2) there is
Divine providence; (3) God is all-powerful; (4) prophecy exists;
(5) humans have free will; and (6) the Torah has a purpose.
Other formulations of basic principles will be considered as appropriate to a discussion. But Jews are not required to believe
in any of these lists of beliefs.

We can talk of God, Torah (God's revelation and teachings),
and Israel (the Jewish people) as the foundation of Judaism,

but it is crucial to remember the basic fact that Judaism does have beliefs and those beliefs separate Judaism from other worldviews, including other religious worldviews. It is similarly important to remember that, very deliberately, those beliefs were purposefully defined in such a way as to allow for large interpretive latitude. Different Jews can have startlingly different interpretations of Judaism and still be following the same belief system. This tolerance of ambiguity is indeed one of the hallmarks of Judaism, a point of pride in offering humans great freedom of thought to ponder the realities of the world.

For example, consider the term *Torah*. In its narrowest meaning, as discussed, the Torah refers to the first five books of the Hebrew Bible. But in a broader sense, Torah is whatever God reveals, however it is revealed. Revelation can come from tradition, from the Jewish community, or, in the view of some, from God to individuals personally.

And yet if Judaism does not have fixed dogmas but does have a worldview, how can we decide what is or is not included in the basic beliefs of Judaism? What are the sources of our understanding of those beliefs? The sources can be considered as coming from several sorts of places. The first place is traditional religious literature. This is supplemented by Jewish theologians and philosophers, Jewish folklore, Jewish culture, and evidence from sources external to Jewish life, such as the natural and social sciences. The sources include:

- The Hebrew Bible, perhaps started as early as the tenth century BCE (before the Common Era) or, according to some views, the sixth century BCE. By tradition, the Torah was given through Moses to the Jewish people at Mount Sinai during the Exodus from Egypt.
- The Mishnah. This code of Jewish law, the first such post-biblical code, and by tradition passed down by Moses, was

put into codified form in about 200 CE (Common Era). It includes the various teachings of Rabbis (a capital R is used to describe these teachers in the Mishnah and Talmud), collectively termed *Tannaim*, who studied and taught during the first two centuries of the Common Era. The Mishnah includes the legal views of those who discussed religious laws.

- The Talmud, the incalculably important collection of Jewish law (Halakhah) and folk stories (Aggadah). There were in fact two separate Talmudim, one in the Land of Israel in about 400 CE and the bigger and more significant one from Babylon in about 500 CE. Generally, the word *Talmud* refers to the Babylonian Talmud, which consists of the Mishnah plus the Gemara, which is made up, in part, of commentaries on the Mishnah by Rabbis who studied and taught from the third to the sixth century CE (the Amoraim). The Amoraim also consider a large number of issues not included in the Mishnah, so it is much more than simply a commentary. For a millennium and a half, the study of Judaism was virtually synonymous, in large part, with the study of the Talmud.

- Collections of Rabbinic Midrash. The word *Midrash* refers to literature that interprets biblical texts. There are many classical compilations of such Rabbinical literature. To cite one example, there are two versions of the Mekhilta, which provides commentary about the Book of Exodus. There are, additionally, compilations of post-Talmudic midrashic commentaries.

- Responsa, meaning "answers," consist of collections of written responses by recognized religious authorities and halachic scholars to a variety of religious questions that have been sent to them. Responsa (the singular is *responsum*) continue to be written until now and form an extensive and intriguing body of Jewish literature.

- Jewish prayer books. These are so important because a prayer book was the way most Jews connected to their religion. For most of Jewish history, prayers, after printing collected into books, were how people understood Judaism.
- Jewish philosophers and theologians. While Maimonides was the great philosopher of the Middle Ages, Jewish philosophy existed before him and had such great figures as Saadia Gaon. It also existed after him. Major post-Maimonidean Jewish philosophers included such people as Gersonides and Hasdai ben Judah Crescas. Other prominent premodern Jewish philosophers included Baruch Spinoza and Jacob Emden. Some of the most influential modern philosophers include Franz Rosenzweig, Martin Buber, Hermann Cohen, and Abraham Joshua Heschel. Contemporary Jewish philosophers include those who study the implications of the Holocaust (such as Emil Fackenheim) and significant issues that have arisen, including Jewish feminism (such as Judith Plaskow).
- Jewish Kabbalistic and mystical texts and traditions.
- Jewish folklore. The folk tales, legends, stories, riddles, and sayings that have been passed on to succeeding Jewish generations can sometimes contain significant clues about Jewish beliefs. Consider, for example, these examples of folk sayings:
  - The highest wisdom is kindness.
  - The face is the worst informer.
  - Better to suffer an injustice than to do an injustice.
  - These three are the marks of a Jew—a tender heart, self-respect, and charity.
  - Don't rejoice at your enemy's fall—but don't rush to pick him up, either.
  - A half-truth is a whole lie.
  - God is closest to those with broken hearts.

- Jewish culture. Basic Jewish beliefs can be found embedded in cultural products such as literature, paintings, and songs. These need to be examined.
- Sources external to Jewish life such as the natural and social sciences. A modern approach to Judaism requires that any sacred beliefs, insofar as possible, be confirmed by objective measures such as the sciences. It is not the case that Jewish beliefs will emerge from the natural or social sciences. Rather, these sciences are used as a reality check when Jewish beliefs include assertions about natural or social realities that have been measured objectively.

The search for the basic beliefs of Judaism does not, then, start with any official religious statement or go to an official religious authority. Those beliefs emerge out of a tradition and a history. Indeed, searching for those basic beliefs is really like looking for a story. This story unfolds with great characters and has a strong narrative. It is a tale filled with intrigue, sadness, and joy. The search for basic Jewish beliefs is a journey into the heart of Judaism—its people, history, and culture; its hopes and fears and dreams.

And so we turn to the beginning of the journey, to a consideration of God.

2

THE MYSTERY OF GOD

Woody Allen put it well: "If only God would give me some clear sign! Like making a large deposit in my name in a Swiss bank." Sadly for us, God is not so inclined. Instead, we have to struggle to find signs of God, to understand what we even mean by the word *God*.

It is an occupational hazard for those of us who write about God and religion that too much of our prose sounds as though we had a hearty conversation-filled dinner with God the night before. It is too often a prose filled with self-assurance about being correct. Religious writers are caught in a conundrum. The truthful admission is that none of us knows the subject we write about. Silence seems the appropriate approach, but silence about God might be interpreted to be a tacit acceptance of atheism or agnosticism and eliminates the power of faith and the sense of God's revelations. For religious Jews, God provides meaning and purpose to lives. Silence therefore makes even less sense than making what are clearly only tentative guesses about the essence of God.

Part of the problem of discussing God is that *God* is a general term that includes a wide range of very different concepts that appear to be similar. The philosopher Ludwig Wittgenstein introduced the term *family resemblances* to such concepts because they have similar appearances but are distinct nevertheless. The different concepts of God have a family resemblance to each other but have no single, central essence. Because of this there is no single definition of God to define God's attributes. Paul Gastwirth, in his essay "Concepts of God," illustrated this cleverly. He noted seven possible concepts (there are, of course, others). He wondered, is God:

Immanent (dwelling within the cosmos) or transcendent (dwelling outside the cosmos)?

Finite or Infinite?

Temporal—that is, evolving—or eternal and unchanging?

Personal and concerned with humans or indifferent to humans?

One Being or many?

A Being or the Ground of Being? (The latter, meaning "Being itself," was a term coined by the Christian existentialist Paul Tillich.)

There are four possible answers to the first question. God might be only immanent, only transcendent, both, or neither. Each of these seven polarities (or opposites) similarly has four possible answers. If we multiply the possibilities, this is the result: $4^7 = 16,384$. That is, just using these polarities, there are more than 16,000 different concepts of God. No wonder talking about God is so imprecise and unclear!

One odd way to look at these statistics is to conclude that everyone is some sort of atheist. After all, if you believe in concept A about God, there are therefore thousands of concepts you don't believe about God. Similarly, an atheist argument about God has the same problem as a theist. The atheist has to explain what concepts are untrue. The realization that there are so many possible definitions of God should also make us realize that even monotheism isn't simply defined. We should also conclude that such a wide variety of alternatives compels us to be tolerant of those with other views, just as we would want them to be tolerant of ours.

So, in keeping with this challenge, we need to define what exactly we mean by God as we discuss Judaism. The Jewish concept of God generally includes the notion that by God we mean a transcendent, infinite, eternal, personal, incorporeal Being as well as one having the other attributes already discussed.

Even with a more precise definition, though, we can still ask: Do we believe in this God Judaism defines? If not, can we consider belief? Nowhere in the Bible is there a command to believe in God. Anyone who is Jewish and thinks deeply and seriously about religious issues is an authentic participant in the Jewish tradition.

Another question is: How do people find God? Or how does God find humans? One answer is through the study of sacred texts or praying. But God is also sometimes found through personal experiences; God for some can be more intimate than abstract ideas and traditions. Consider Tevye the milkman in the musical *Fiddler on the Roof*. Tevye spends his day talking to God as though God were a friendly coworker. Tevye also makes up Bible verses that miraculously match his own views. But he can be forgiven. Tevye is not learned, but he is genuinely Jewish. For him, God is a companion, not an object of belief. God can, according to some thinkers, also be found through pure reason and logic.

Medieval Jewish thinkers, for example, convinced that logic could provide a proof of God, maintained that it was a duty to use our reason to construct such a proof. Such use of reason was considered worthwhile. After all, if you could prove to your satisfaction that God existed, the medievalists thought, you would inoculate yourself against subsequent doubt. You would clarify and in general more deeply understand your ideas about God. Your efforts had the valuable side benefit of increasing your reasoning skills to be used in other areas of your life.

There have been various purely logical arguments put forward to argue that God exists. Take a couple of examples. The cosmological argument is that there had to be a beginning of the cosmos. God is the first cause, the prime mover, the reason why there is something rather than nothing. The moral argument is that humans have a sense of right and wrong, that some actions ought to be taken and some actions ought not. Where, it was asked, did this sense come from if not from God?

This is not to argue that unbelievers are immoral or amoral, but that moral judgments become a matter of personal belief or received social conditioning rather than from objective standards outside human judgment. Put in a dramatic form, we can ask: Was Hitler immoral? Without an objective response, we are left with the emotion that he was a mad mass murderer, but is that any more than a personal or historical decision, or is it an objectively moral one?

There is also the logical argument from people having had subjective, profound religious experiences. Since these experiences occurred to so many people in so many places over such an expansive amount of time, the argument goes, doesn't that show that there really is a God? The flaw of the argument is that many people across time and region can simply be wrong about a subject, such as that the Earth is flat or that slavery is an acceptable practice.

Beyond reason, we can approach God by a deep sense of connection to a sacred reality, a deep belief in the existence of goodness.

Our personal experience might prompt us to make what the existentialists call a leap of faith, a personal, fateful decision that we will believe. The existentialists thought those who relied on reason alone were only taking part of a human's capacity for faith into account. Instead, the existentialists argued, it is the entire human who responds, the entire human who seeks a relationship with God. The existentialist does not take a leap into the dark void, hoping to land in faith. It is a leap from belief to a deeper emotional state, from reason to a full emotional commitment to and relationship with God.

Like everyone else, the existentialist is caught in the human condition. Doubt is an ever-present alternative to faith, always wandering nearby, closer than ever on the dark nights of painful experiences. We always are in the process of choosing whether or not to believe, and we always have to use our intuition about which choice is correct.

This existentialist approach is very congenial to the Biblical view. There are no logical proofs of God attempted in the Hebrew Bible. Instead, as we see in such figures as Abraham, Moses, and the Prophets, God is approached with deep passion, faith, concern, and duty, not only with the mind.

For some people, being religious means having a particular personal experience. For many, that experience may be compared to aesthetic experiences, being overwhelmed, for instance, by the beauty of a sunset. For many people, encountering the overwhelming wonder of a new birth, of a startling sunrise, of fresh air after a rain can be enough to ignite and define a relationship with God.

For some, this feeling of wonder and awe translates also into a feeling of powerlessness in the presence of the vast cosmos, or the desire for the greatness of God to absorb the nothingness of the human.

Using reason, the leap of faith, and mystical experiences, individuals find their own way to faith. There are many possible approaches.

Study is another source of inspiration. Reading beautiful prose about God like the Biblical psalms or Abraham Joshua Heschel's stunning book *God in Search of Man* can lead to considerations of God.

Some people pray, and in talking to God and listening for the "still, small voice" within, the promptings of an informed conscience, they are led to a sense of inner peace and a powerful connection to a transcendent Being.

Others engage in religious rituals, or social action to improve the world, or learn from the holiness in other people, or find models of belief in Jewish history.

We might also approach God on the basis of a religious tradition, an acknowledgment that our ancestors were in touch with religious truth and passed it on to us. We identify with our ancestors and want to honor them. More basically, in Judaism we acknowledge in adhering to tradition that God gave the Jewish people a revelation through an incursion into history at Mount Sinai and the giving of the Torah. For contemporary Jews, the whole issue of the divine nature of biblical authorship is much more troubling than it was for our ancestors. Modern scholars have provided convincing proofs that the Bible is of human authorship, so we have to consider what that means for our accepting tradition, even as we acknowledge that the God encountered at Sinai endowed untold generations of Jews with a moral charge, a set of commandments worth dying for because they so deeply infused life with meaning.

This Jewish tradition teaches us about God with philosophical and theological speculation, personal experience, divine actions, and God's revelations. These are understood in widely varying ways within that tradition. There are Jewish movements that deny the existence of a supernatural God and understand the idea of God in a new and nontraditional way. There are Jewish members of movements that accept the idea of a supernatural God but do not themselves believe in God. That is, there is no universally accepted belief about God. Below is a description of a traditional belief and some modern concerns and interpretations.

The obvious should be noted. Humans lack the language and the logical capacity to have a full understanding of God. We rely on faith more than on knowledge, but in Judaism's case, it is a faith that has persisted across time and continents, a faith that has adapted to new knowledge and understanding, and a faith that prizes wrestling with its own beliefs.

For example, modern Jews have finally taken notice of the enormous role Jewish women have played in Jewish history and how that notice affects our understanding of Jewish thought. We now, for example, have to emphasize that God is not a male or female. For that matter, God is neither black nor white, or a member of a particular religion or ethnic group. We are all equal reflections of God. We now recognize that Jewish religious denominations arose to confront historical modernity, not because one or the other reflects a true understanding of God.

As Judith Plaskow notes in her groundbreaking book *Standing Again at Sinai*, as Moses prepared the Israelites to receive the Torah he told them (Exodus 19:15), "Be ready for the third day, do not go near a woman." Plaskow concludes that such a view denies women even a presence on Mount Sinai, and, by implication, in Jewish religious tradition generally. Plaskow's is a crucial observation and a prompt that as we discuss God, we not picture either a male or female figure, and as we talk about Jewish history and the evolution of Jewish thought we need a

constant reminder that if male thinkers are being discussed it is
because women were systematically disallowed from contributing or even participating in the ongoing theological enterprise.
As in the case of thinking about God, we also need to consider
how Jewish religious beliefs and Jewish history can be newly
understood by considering a feminist perspective.

The Jewish revolution in history was to introduce the world
to a unified God outside Nature, filled with boundless creative
power, and with a moral personality and a moral will. There
had been earlier experiments in monotheism, the belief in one
God, but Judaism's was unique in adding a moral dimension
and in providing a view that was sustained over time so that
it had incalculably powerful influences in human history that
resonate to today. The Jewish view was, of course, presented
in the Bible. The various people who wrote the Bible, and the
editor who pieced it all together, were not searching for a proof
of God's existence. God's presence was, for them, as real and
obvious as the rain that fell, the flowers that bloomed, and the
churning emotions that drove their desires and their hopes. The
Bible writers knew God as an immediate part of their religious
consciousness. And while Biblical religion stressed the ethical
conception of the personality of God, a fuller idea emerges from
Jewish sacred literature, thoughtful examination, and history.

The Jewish understanding of God begins with the basic fact
of God's existence.

EXISTENCE

The Jewish belief system starts with God, and thoughts of God
rightfully begin with the simple assertion that God is real, not
a projection of the human imagination, not a fanciful childlike
delusion, but a genuine entity. It is a reasonable question, but an

unanswerable one, to ask: From where or what did God emerge? To ask the question is to come up against the limits of human logic. Either there was a creative first force of some sort, God, a vacuum, some natural force, or there wasn't. Either alternative is difficult for us to grasp. For every first force we can conceive, we can infinitely ask: What caused that seeming first force? But the alternative is equally difficult to grasp, namely that there was no first force, that all the cosmos just appeared without a first force. Note that this is not a matter of gaining more scientific knowledge, for we can always ask, for example, why that scientific first force exists. That is, perhaps unsurprisingly, God is an unexplainable mystery, a mystery that in principle lies outside the powers of human consciousness to grasp. We use the term *God* to refer to that first force. Of course, God has a lot more for us to understand, but existence is the beginning. We can't prove God exists. We can't prove God doesn't exist. But we can state that our understanding of the idea of God includes existence.

UNITY: GOD IS ONE

God's unity is so central to the Jewish conception of God that Maimonides listed it as the second of his Thirteen Principles, placed only after God's existence. Unity is the center of the Sh'ma, Judaism's most defining declaration, usually translated in such words as "Hear O Israel, the Lord is Our God, the Lord is One" (Deuteronomy 6:4).

Asserting that God is one is simultaneously to assert that God is not all else. God is not none, as the reality of God's existence indicates. God is not two, like the Manichean belief that an evil being has an equivalent amount of power as a good God and the two are perpetually fighting. God is not three, as Christianity might be interpreted. (Formally, Christianity claims to be monotheistic and that the three parts, the Father, Son, and Holy Spirit, are all part of the same God; one linguistic distinction might be to call Judaism "pure monotheism.") And, finally, to say that God is one is to say that God is not many, as pagans did.

The concept of God's unity includes a cluster of interrelated ideas:

1. God is the single supreme entity. *Entity* is sometimes used instead of *being* because God is not a being. Sometimes it is impossible to describe God without resorting to human analogies. The Bible, after all, does this, but when possible it should be avoided as a reminder that God is not conceived in the same physical, psychological, or any other way as a human is. Still, for the sake of clarity, *being* will sometimes be employed. The point here is that while God exists, no other gods exist.
2. God is unique in that no comparable entities exist.
3. Because God is unique and singular, no other entity should be worshipped. God is not the Supreme God among other gods also worthy of worship. That is the difference between monotheism, worshipping a single united God, and monolatry, worshipping the most powerful among several gods.
4. God cannot be divided into smaller entities. God is indivisible.
5. God has no extraneous elements or parts and lacks no other elements or parts. In this sense, unity means God is complete as is.
6. A united God can create a united cosmos. This sounds abstract, but science could not have arisen without a monotheistic conception of God. Science, after all, asserts a single unified system of laws that explains nature. Polytheism, the idea of many gods, would have precluded such a scientific conception.

7. Maimonides pointed out that God's unity means God can't have plural moral dispositions or attributes. This complicates ordinary language. For example, as is being done in this chapter, it is common to talk of God as knowing all, being all good, and so on. But a unified God can't have plural attributes, and so such language is inadequate to describe God even if humans have no other way to do so.

8. Unity implies a harmony between polarities, seemingly opposite concepts such as conforming and being an individual, love and fear, obligations to the self and obligations to the community, being religious and being spiritual, being loyal to the Jewish people and being loyal to all humanity, among many others.

The unity of God also stands as a metaphor for dealing with polarities. A united concept that brings together aspects of these polarities draws upon each of them and puts them together proportionally. Unity can be understood as combining or arranging both parts into a whole.

Where humans see opposites, the notion of unity implies an ultimate harmony. Indeed, the word *shalom*, which often is translated as a welcome or a wish for peace is more usefully understood as implying a harmony that is the opposite of chaos. God represents that harmony.

Harmony does not necessarily imply splitting the difference between two opposites, or finding some mean between them. A balanced mean between two polarities might not be truthful or just. In an argument between a democrat and a Nazi, anyone whose goal is to find a delicate balance violates truth and decency. Still, the notion of God's unity as providing a lesson for humans is important. An idea of unity implies that, when possible, a moderation in life and an attempt, when morally possible, to find reason and harmony is a good guide to living.

The unity of God is so foundational to Judaism that it is part of its definition. Judaism has therefore been defined as ethical monotheism.

There are those who see the development of monotheism as negative. Freud thought a belief in one God inevitably led to religious intolerance. Others went further and thought that monotheism led to a distinction between a true religion and all the rest and that distinction gave birth to violence and persecution.

No one can deny that religion has led to an enormous amount of violence in human history, and insofar as a religion has a belief system that is thought to be uniquely true, especially if that belief system is seen as required for salvation, it is possible to see how such an idea could be used to justify intolerance and its consequences.

But intolerance is caused by any totalitarianism system. Nazism and Communism, not religious in any traditional sense, led to the death and suffering of tens of millions of people.

However, monotheism, especially the monotheism that Judaism developed, is not by definition intolerant. This is because there is no official Jewish belief system, so Judaism couldn't see itself as uniquely true. Gentiles were not required to become Jewish in order to achieve salvation. Even in ancient times, when Judaism, Christianity, and paganism all existed in the Roman Empire, the Jews, according to Jonathan Kirsch, "found a way to carry on the worship of the God of Israel throughout the Diaspora without disturbing (or being disturbed by) their pagan neighbors."

OMNIPOTENCE

The idea of God being all-powerful is a gateway concept to understanding much else, including the creation of the cosmos and the problem of evil. We usually understand omnipotence to mean that God is capable of all. Being all-powerful means that there was no matter or substance that preceded God from which God was made, that there is no power anywhere in the cosmos that is not ultimately dependent on God's omnipotent power, and that God can exercise power in every way that God chooses to do so. In Genesis 18:1–15, for example, Abraham is told that Sarah, his ninety-year-old wife, is going to give birth. Sarah laughs at the idea, but then the reply comes: "Is anything too hard for the Lord?" The Biblical assertion is that God is capable of all, even that which is seemingly beyond reason.

But this notion is more complicated than it seems. We read the Bible through modern eyes, the eyes of a scientifically informed world, a world with a long tradition of philosophical thinking. It is, however, crucial to recall that the Bible does not seek to prove postulates in the way, say, Greek philosophy did. The Bible's conception of God's omnipotence shouldn't be seen through modern eyes.

The Bible is a moral document, filled with cautionary tales aimed at ethical guidance. It is not history, or science, or theology. God's power is not the power of performance but the power of moral persuasion. What this means is that as we consider omnipotence we will have to change the standard understanding of it.

It was only under the influence of Greek philosophy that medieval Jewish thinkers began to ponder logical questions with apparent contradictions such as: Can God create a stone God can't lift? Some of these thinkers, such as Saadia and Joseph Albo, concluded that God could do what seems to us physically impossible but God could not do what is logically impossible (e.g., make a square triangle).

Another way of looking at this is to consider God before the creation of the cosmos and after its creation. Before the cosmos came into being, God could do all that God wished to do, but the creation of the cosmos included physical laws and logical propositions that created time and space. In that natural cosmos, God could not do the logically impossible and God could not alter time, such as by changing the past.

For those who believe in miracles, God can alter the physical laws of the cosmos. But does that mean that God's creation was imperfect? In the Talmud, this dilemma was answered by the claim that all the miracles recorded in the Bible were preordained at the world's beginning. For those moderns who don't believe in miracles, God has maximal power but is limited (or self-limited since God created the cosmos) within the natural world. Of course, after the Temple was destroyed by the Romans and the people scattered, even the most religious wondered why such a calamity occurred if God is omnipotent.

This question has haunted Jewish history. The modern notion of a limited God who does not intrude in history provides a sort of explanation, but such a notion of a limited God is outside the Jewish traditional view and, in many ways, is not religiously satisfying. Who wants a God that can't intervene to save a baby from disaster or cure a terminally ill child? This dilemma runs through many of the issues confronting religion and will thematically recur in various Jewish beliefs. That is, neither the traditional view nor the modern, more limited notion comes without serious problems, as we will discover.

OMNISCIENCE

Jewish holy texts conceived of God as all-knowing. That is, within the cosmos and the limits of human logic, the term *all-knowing* means that God knows all knowable knowledge. "He knows what is in the darkness, and the light dwells with

Him" (Daniel 2:22). "Although God is in the heavens, His eyes behold and search the sons of man" (Exodus Rabbah, 2:2). Traditional Jewish religious leaders understood God's omniscience as applying to the past and present but also to the future. The famous Talmudic scholar Rabbi Akiba, trying to leave room for human freedom, asserted that "All is foreseen, but freedom of choice is given" (Avot 3:16). The dilemma inherent in the idea that humans had free will despite God's foreknowledge provided great difficulties for medieval Jewish philosophers. They came to a variety of potential solutions. Maimonides accepted the standard idea that humans retained their freedom despite God's complete knowledge of the future. Gersonides differed. He thought humans were free, but that meant that God was incapable of having complete knowledge of future human actions. Crescas took the final logical alternative. He believed that free will was an illusion because God has complete knowledge of all human actions.

Maimonides's view may grate on the modern ear, but such a position allows for the idea of God to see and understand all and therefore to be in a position to be a judge of human intention and behavior. It is a position that preserves the human intuition that we have free will. But it doesn't solve the logical contradiction that God knows what free people will do. Tempting as it is to follow Gersonides, it should be noted that a belief in free will and God's being limited in foreknowledge has significant religious implications. Because if humans are free and God does not know what humans will do, then it becomes difficult to discern God's purpose in creating humans. They might, with their free will, do whatever they wanted when they wanted to do it. They wouldn't necessarily follow God's commands and ethical rules, and if they wouldn't do that, it is not clear why God would have created people in the first place, how their purpose of the cosmos is to be understood, and the nature of the goal of human existence. Additionally, as will be considered below, the rise of neuroscience, cognitive psychology, and brain research has brought with it claims by some that free will is an illusion (along with the illusion of a supernatural God).

But, in the modern sense, just as God only has the power to do what is possible, so God only has the knowledge to know what is knowable. God can't know the answer to the question "When will God die?" because that possibility doesn't exist.

There is another, more useful, approach to God's knowledge and that is to make a distinction between knowledge of what actions humans will take and wisdom about actions humans should take. Wisdom includes having good judgment, being discreet and prudent, correctly evaluating the significance of knowledge, and perspective and insight on the meaning of knowledge. If wisdom rather than the specific knowledge of future events is the meaning of omniscience, then God can remain omniscient without knowing the future and humans can still be free.

ETERNAL

God, according to Jewish tradition, is outside time, is indeed the creator of time. And while the cosmos (and time) had a beginning, popularly known as the Big Bang, approximately 13.75 billion years ago, God is not measured by that occurrence. God is always there. The Talmud notes, "Everything decays, but You do not decay." The point of this assertion is that, unlike all in the created cosmos, God does not change or erode. God, already being perfect, could not in principle change, for to change implies that perfectibility had not been achieved and change was needed or that God was perfect and changed, making God no longer perfect.

There is a bit of a philosophical difficulty in such an approach, however. For if God created the cosmos, which was affected by time and change, then God, in the act of creating, changed to become a creator or, if God's essential nature remained unchanged, then God's relations with what was outside God changed with the creation of a cosmos.

A belief in God's perfection implies, perhaps, that God did not need to create the cosmos and was complete without it but because of purpose or love or some such motivation God created the cosmos, which had no ultimate effect on God's timelessness or perfection. Human logic runs up against the idea of God as timeless, and our logic falls short. We perceive through our senses, and God has no senses. We have a human brain, and God does not. We live in space and God is outside it. (The technical term is *spacetime*, but, for clarity's sake, the popular term is used.) The human perception, then, is not only different from God's but also incapable of truly apprehending it.

OMNIPRESENCE

The notion of omniscience is not always well understood. As Homer once said to God on the cartoon show *The Simpsons*, "You're everywhere. You're omnivorous."

Beyond being a unified, single entity, God is nonphysical, or incorporeal. That is, God is not made of any of the forms or substances in nature and God's Being is not limited by space. As Psalms 148:13 puts it, God's "glory is over the earth and heaven." Here, again, the Bible is helping us understand God by using human terms. Borrowing human terms assists our understanding of God. As a nonphysical Being, God is not in space, but God's presence or spirit is felt in all of space. It is a psychological not a physical presence.

TRANSCENDENCE AND IMMINENCE

The problem of understanding God in time has a companion problem: understanding God in space. The Big Bang created space, and God does not reside in space. We humans are trapped by our language. To talk of God as transcendent, as outside space, is difficult to conceive, for we can make the error of thinking of God as above the cosmos—that is, applying a spatial term when no such term is appropriate. But it is not a Jewish notion that God is only (to use another inadequate spatial term) beyond the cosmos. Deism is the view that God is exclusively beyond the cosmos and therefore can have no interaction with or continuing effect on humans. In contrast, pantheism is the view that God is only imminent, only part of the cosmos and not separate from it. Spinoza is perhaps the most famous Jewish pantheist; he conceived of God and nature as identical. Judaism's view is that God is both transcendent and imminent, existing beyond the universe but choosing to work within it as well. This seeming contradiction was expressed by the great medieval philosopher and poet Judah Halevi in a poem:

> Lord, where shall I find thee?
> High and hidden is thy place.
> And where shall I not find thee?
> The world is full of thy glory.

It should also be noted that the Hasidic movement in Judaism, especially the Chabad variety, believes more precisely in panentheism, the mystical view that God simultaneously penetrates all that is in the natural world and all that is beyond it. Some Jewish theists thought this view heretical, suggesting that it argues there is only God and that natural substances are not independent of God. The problem, as more traditional supernaturalists argued, is that the panentheistic view destroys the significant distinctions between what is holy and what is not and ultimately obliterates the distinction between good and evil.

PERSONAL

In the Bible and subsequent texts, God is portrayed as having a personal relationship with humans. God gives them commandments. God engages in self-revelation with Abraham, Moses, and others and with the entire Israelite people at Mount Sinai. God makes promises to the Israelites based on their willingness to follow the commandments. God provides guidance, help, and divine intervention. God is depicted as having lots of sides to the divine personality. God is sometimes portrayed as warm and kind and at other times as stern and judgmental. God, that is, was ascribed characteristics seen in humans, such as fathers and rulers, as though this Supreme Being were simply a larger-than-life person.

Perhaps the most famous modern Jewish conception of God as personal was made by Martin Buber in his influential work *I and Thou*. There were several incidents in his life that affected his outlook. One of these incidents occurred while Buber was at the beginning of his scholarly career. He was at home working on a manuscript when he was interrupted by someone knocking on his door. The man there was clearly upset, but Buber's mind was on the manuscript that needed work. Buber was brusque with the man, responding insufficiently, or, as the philosopher later put it, "I did not answer the questions which he did not ask." A few days after this visit the anxious man died, evidently by committing suicide. This tragic event led Buber to realize that his encounters with people were more important than his scholarship or his philosophical musings.

In *I and Thou*, Buber defines an I-It relationship as one in which we view objects or people through the lens of how we use them. We don't see them as full people. Consider a playboy and a woman. The playboy meets, uses, and throws away the woman, then looks for another woman. This is entirely an I-It relationship. In an I-Thou relationship, the other person is an equal, as fully a person as the I doing the meeting.

For Buber, we can't talk about God but to God. The question for him is not "Does God exist?" but "What does God have to say to me?"

For Buber, whenever we have an I-Thou relationship we are meeting God, for God is the ultimate Thou. Thus Buber emphasizes how we meet God, not any metaphysical attributes of God.

The notion of a personal God is absolutely crucial to Judaism, for without it there is no revelation of God's purpose, no divine mission, no meaning. This will unfold as we consider humans and how they as persons react to God's personal nature.

MORALITY

Judaism's unique historical contribution to thinking about God is seen in the conception of God as moral, fiercely moral. God is understood as purely good, passionate about justice, and appropriately merciful. God is a model of goodness as well as its source. When we see good in others and when we act with goodness ourselves, that is seen as a reflection of God. The Talmud often suggests that the conflict between justice and mercy is an eternal one, with God ready for both. This realization led the Rabbis who participated in the discussions recorded in the Talmud to stress repentance so as to merit mercy.

The understanding of God as good, however, inevitably leads to the question of the existence of evil in the world, a discussion undertaken at length in chapter 4. The discussion of evil rests on the foundation of understanding God. Jewish tradition has it that God, while purely God, nonetheless created evil (Isaiah 45:7). The dilemma for people rests precisely on this idea. For if God is all-good and all-powerful, and evil is real and not an illusion, the dilemma of evil is powerful. If evil is real and God cannot eliminate it (or not have created it originally) then God, by the traditional definition, is not all-powerful. If God chooses not to do so, then how can God be considered all-good? More basically, why did a perfect God create an imperfect world? That is the Jewish conundrum about God that humans have to consider.

But God's moral nature is the defining characteristic. Judaism is not just monotheism, but ethical monotheism.

HOLY

In the Bible, the seraphim, or heavenly beings, sing this song: "Holy, holy, holy, is the Lord of hosts; The whole Earth is full of His glory" (Isaiah 6:3). God's holiness rests on a separation from the material world, the profane, and so whatever is associated with God is considered holy, such as the ancient Temples or the synagogues of today.

God's holiness means that any approach to God must be made in the spirit of being holy. Inherent in such a notion is the crucial idea that it is possible for all people to be holy.

PURPOSEFULNESS

The very fact of the existence of the cosmos is a powerful indication that God had a purpose. As we shall see, the fact that it is an imperfect cosmos, one filled with accidents and physical terror such as disease and disasters, also implies that humans have a purpose in partnership with God. Of course, humans can't know God's purposes, but we can try to infer that there are purposes. So we might conclude that there is purpose in the creation of a natural world, in the creation of humans, in the election of the Jewish people to be a holy people, in God's revelation to humanity, and in the general effort of humans to fulfill their own moral tasks.

Purpose must mean that God has a goal in mind (redemption), a means to achieve the goal (the divine teachings), and a moral teacher charged with focusing on the goal (the Jewish people).

God's ethical purpose starts with the initial Godly interaction with the natural world: the creation of the cosmos.

EXERCISES

The exercise section in each chapter is meant as place for suggestions about how readers can leap from this book to experiences. For each chapter, I suggest starting by looking over the bibliography in the back of this book and doing some additional reading.

I wrote a lot about awe and wonder in this chapter. Reading traditional Jewish texts is a good way to understand the Jewish experience with awe. I enjoy reading the Psalms, for example. Many Jews study the Talmud each day. Others read Jewish news in papers or online or enjoy novels or films about Jewish life, or sing or dance to Jewish music. Some visit a sacred Jewish space. Perhaps you can visit a famous synagogue or, if you're lucky, go to the Western Wall in Jerusalem.

I hope you'll consider the experiences that make you feel as though the cosmos is big and beautiful.

Beyond reading and visiting places—and perhaps the most powerful—is to connect to awe through human beings. I felt overwhelming awe, for example, when I was present at the birth of our four children, when I held them and wondered what could possibly be going on in their minds. Similarly, holding my grandchildren made me feel as though I was holding all the past and all the future.

Consider the people who might be wondrous to you. Maybe a special date with a loved one or a visit to a sibling or friend you haven't seen in a while.

To make this experience religious, seek to feel the presence of God in that moment of wonder, to sense a power there with you that you connect to through that awe.

Prayer is a frequently traveled path to experiencing God. I had a serious health problem in 2011, and among the many messages I received was this extraordinary one from Rabbi Benjamin Blech, a noted author and scholar. It is reprinted with his approval.

I can tell you from personal experience that prayer very often has a positive effect—not only your own prayers for a speedy recovery but I firmly believe the prayers of those motivated for whatever reason to pray on your behalf can make a difference. . . . I am not a mystic nor an unrealistic dreamer. Yet, close to half century in the rabbinate has proven to me that God works in wondrous ways and that communicating with Him in ways that make clear that a person's continued stay on this Earth is meaningful to others can be the key to divine intervention and care. So I will pray for you because in ways unknown to you, you have touched me through your books. Allow me to add one more thing that I have learnt. Whatever doctors tell you is but one part of the equation. Our physical diagnosis obviously plays a great role. But at least equal in importance is our mental and emotional attitude. I urge you to be optimistic. Optimism is the flipside of faith. In all my years of experience, almost all of those who gave up created self-fulfilling prophecies. Conversely, the people who truly believed they would be well either achieved it on their own through their optimism or gave God good reason to grant them more years to serve as spokesmen for their positive attitude to life. You have much to live for. I convey to you my blessings, my prayers and my hope.

There are many traditional prayers to say. As discussed above in the section on unity, many people recite a line from the Sh'ma prayer taken from the Bible, Deuteronomy 6:4:

Sh'ma Yisrael, Adonai Eloheynu, Adonai echad.
Hear O Israel, the Lord is Our God, the Lord is One.

You can pray in a synagogue or alone. You can pray in any language, though Hebrew has a unique character when it comes to prayer.

You can pray when you're grateful, or scared, or seek guidance and insights.

Prayer is such a personal activity, such a quiet, contemplative moment that the experience of it is too subtle for language.

Prayer can be a monologue, with you doing all the praying or your reading a prayer book or the Bible with God "speaking."

But prayer can also be a dialogue, in which you talk and listen to the still, small voice within you or observe the world looking for clues to lead you to interpret what God means to convey to you.

In prayer, silence can be the most eloquent sound.

Consider when you feel close to God. Make a list. This might include, for example, being present at the birth of a child, or on a holy day, or when you are singing. But also consider when you feel distant from God, such as when someone good dies young, or when you read about some tragedy or a great tragedy such as the Holocaust.

Think of moments when you needed to have hope. Consider what closeness to God would have felt like or did feel like.

Make a list of questions you would ask God if you could.

Consider what is at stake in your beliefs. Rabbi Abraham Joshua Heschel put this very well: "God is of no importance unless He is of supreme importance."

3

THE CREATION OF THE WORLD

Rabbi Hillel is one of the most famous sages in the Talmud. He imparted a remarkable amount of wisdom, including this statement: "Even if I knew that I would die tomorrow, I would still plant an apple tree today." This thought represents more than a belief that even in death he could contribute to the lives of others. His statement represents a profound faith in the natural order, that despite the fact that he was gone the apple tree would continue to grow and yield its fruit. Ultimately, Hillel is expressing his belief that God's world is a good one and that humans should put their faith in it.

GOD AND CREATION

It is a basic traditional Jewish belief that God is the creator of the cosmos. The word *cosmos* comes from the same Greek root as the word *cosmetic* and means "arrangement" or "adornment." In this book, *cosmos* is used as synonymous with the universe or all of material reality that there is in this universe.

But why did God create the cosmos? If God is a perfect Being, why was it necessary to add to God's existence? If perfect, God didn't need a world. The only seeming response to this question is that God created the cosmos for a reason, a purpose. Ultimately the purpose involved human beings, but human beings had to live somewhere. Given this purpose, God's creation of the world could not just be an artistic, creative endeavor. There was an ultimate moral plan.

Creation ends the unity of the reality that existed before the cosmos. After the creation, there is a non-God part of reality. Creation gives birth to the idea of there existing more than one part of cosmic unity even while God's unity remains. Cosmic diversity had been born and with it the idea that God is both being and becoming, both continuity and change.

A cosmogony is a theory about the universe's birth. The Bible's cosmogony rests on two stories at the beginning of Genesis. The Torah opens with the first creation story in Genesis 1:1–2:4: "When God began to create heaven and earth—the earth being unformed and void, with darkness over the surface of the deep and a wind from God sweeping over the water— God said, 'Let there be light'; and there was light." The second Genesis story is in 2:4–24 in which God forms humans from the dust of the Earth. Note that there are preexisting elements in the world; God didn't create the cosmos out of nothing but from the chaos of earth and water. In later terms, creation from nothing came to be called, especially in non-Jewish theology, creatio ex nihilo.

Early Christianity developed a new cosmogony that there was no material in the world prior to creation. That became part of Islamic theology, and through it creation from nothing found its way to medieval Jewish theology.

SCIENCE AND CREATION

Eventually science came along to challenge the religious world-view on two levels. The first level was on a literal reading of the Bible, and the second, related to that, was whether it was God or some natural force that created the world. Most modern thinkers have abandoned what traditionalists still believe: that God gave the Torah to Moses at Mount Sinai. A standard contemporary view is that the Bible is not cosmology but literature. It uses stories, traditions, and poetic devices such as metaphors to provide an epic for the Jewish people. As such, its purpose is to discuss folk beliefs, not science, and to transmit a moral vision, a sense of personal and communal values, not provide a literal description, including offering a poetic description of the creation of the world.

This sounds pleasing to the modern ear, but this point of view is not without problems. If religion doesn't have to do with cosmology, then Judaism is not about all of reality. That doesn't mean someone who thinks God created the world has to accept the biblical account, however. It's possible that God used scientific laws to create material reality and that while creation is a religious and not a physical doctrine, physical laws become subsumed under religious ones.

The idea that God brought natural laws into existence to create the natural world in some sense coheres with traditional Judaism. On this account, these laws form an agreement with the world, a foreshadowing of the covenants God would make with all humans (symbolized by a rainbow) and then just with the Jewish people. In the Bible, this is expressed in Jeremiah 33:25–26: "Thus said the Lord: As surely as I have established My covenant with day and night—the laws of heaven and earth—so I will never reject the offspring of Jacob and My servant David."

There is a crucial problem with this approach. If God created the laws, such as those that humans have designated as physics and quantum mechanics, was creation a one-time event? That is, did God just let natural forces occur according to their prescribed rules and withhold any further involvement with the cosmos? Such a position, called Deism, begs the question of why such a God should be worshipped, or how is it possible to consider that God good or to have a moral relationship with that God or how to seek guidance or any sort of revelation from that God.

For all these reasons, the vast majority of Jewish thinkers reject Deism. Those who believe in a supernatural God believe in a moral God, a Being involved with humanity. Indeed, the twentieth-century influential Jewish philosopher Franz Rosenzweig believed creation was an ongoing process, that we humans have no existence apart from God, and so we depend on God. For Rosenzweig it is precisely this dependence that leads us to God's revelation.

But many cosmologists like Stephen Hawking reject the idea of a God above nature. According to the standard model of creation, some force triggered the Big Bang. The event itself seems to create various questions to which we do not have answers.

For example, it seems obvious to ask what happened before the Big Bang. The scientific answer seems like a deceptive magic trick to many people. As it happens, the Big Bang created time itself. There is therefore no such concept as "before" the Big Bang because "before" implies the existence of time. We simply don't have a language to discuss a question like this. Maybe we could designate *Time-1* to mean what ordinary people refer to when they ask what happened before the Big Bang. At any rate, the painful answer is, we don't know. It turns out that the world is not a riddle but a mystery. A riddle, after all, has an answer. We never learn the answer to the world. We learn only the limits of our knowledge, not the finished facts of the world. Facts can be confined by language or mathematical representations. The world's mystery eludes such confinements, making writing about the world particularly challenging.

Because the Big Bang created time, the related question, What caused the Big Bang? also has no answer. There was no such entity as causation, which is a time-related phenomenon.

We could also ask: What exploded in the Big Bang? The Big Bang created matter. Where did the Big Bang occur? And there's the same problem. The Big Bang created space. There was no "there" before space was created. Again we might designate a new word, *Space-1*, to refer to what in ordinary language is meant by space in a (to use a scientifically nonsensical phrase) pre–Big Bang world. The answer to the question of where was the Big Bang is everywhere.

A modern Jew might define God as identical to the Big Bang, but, like an identification of God with nature (a position called pantheism and advocated by such thinkers as Spinoza and, according to some, Einstein), such an identity has lost touch with Judaism's crucial understanding of the cosmos having a moral dimension. For mainstream Jewish thinkers, the idea of nature had to be separated from the idea of God in order to have moral progress.

Some theists, seizing on the seeming similarity between the Big Bang, and the biblical moment of creation, see the event as providing some proof of God. But it doesn't. However, it also doesn't rule out God.

Other theists see what is sometimes called a fine-tuned universe. This means that various physical constants are and have to be within a very narrow range for the cosmos to exist. If they were only slightly different, then the cosmos would not have produced life because the environment life requires would not exist.

For example, if the Earth were 5 percent closer to the sun, the temperatures on Earth, as on Venus, would reach 900 degrees Fahrenheit. If we were 20 percent farther away from the sun, we would be covered by a carbon dioxide cloud and be frozen, the way Mars is. If the gravitational force constant were larger, stars would be so hot and burn so rapidly that chemical elements needed for life would not form. If the constant were smaller, stars would be so cool they couldn't ignite nuclear fusion and, again, many of life's needed elements wouldn't form. Some theists accept that there are more than thirty examples of a fine-tuned universe.

According to what is called the Anthropic Principle, such a universe inevitably leads to life and, to some theists at least, adds further evidence of the existence of God.

But, as nontheists are quick to point out, the structure of the cosmos does not prove there is a God. According to the multiverse theory, for example, there are many universes that have different physical constants. Given the variation, some are conducive to life and some are not. Obviously, these theorists posit, we live in a universe that does promote life.

Beyond the physics of cosmology, there are other scientific aspects of creation that seem to challenge a religious interpretation. Quantum mechanics is one of these. The cosmos works, according to the laws of quantum mechanics, on the scale of the very small. A major problem for scientists is the Uncertainty Principle as explained by Werner Heisenberg. According to this principle, we can't know the precise position and the precise direction and speed of a particular particle, a small constituent of matter, at the same time. Because of this we have to assign an imprecise quantum state, a probability of a particle's position and movement. That is, we can never determine, say, where an electron is in relation to the nucleus of an atom. To put it in a disturbingly stark form: reality is random and immeasurable.

This fact was famously unnerving to Einstein, who wrote in a letter: "The theory [of quantum mechanics] says a lot, but does not really bring us any closer to the secret of the 'Old One.' I, at any rate, am convinced that He is not playing at dice."

Poor Einstein. He frequently referred to God as the "Old One," but thought like all the scientists who preceded him that natural order was the primary principle of the natural world. Indeed, many earlier scientists believed in such a rigid adherence to law that they saw the universe as a place of mechanical determinism. But quantum mechanics undermines such a view. On a subatomic level there is no determined certainty. Note that it's not a matter of difficulty; it's not that, for example, we simply don't yet have the instruments or skills to measure an electron but one day we might be able to do so. That is what is so difficult for the mind to grasp, so at odds with common sense. The electrons do not have a specific location. The universe is random.

This sounds as though there can't be any intended outcome by a God in creating the world. But, to follow Einstein's metaphor, dice are more complex than that. A gambling casino runs according to chance. There's no guarantee that any particular roll of the dice or the turning over of any card will result in a win for the gambler or the house. The gambling, like the cosmos, is random. And yet at the end, despite the genuine randomness, the house always wins. They make a profit. The casino has it set up so that statistically, over time—not because of any one spin of the roulette wheel, but over the course of the day—they will win. Similarly, it's possible that the cosmos was set up to be genuinely random but structured so that over time life would emerge. Indeed, such a view has additional implications for the notion of evil. Sometimes in a gambling establishment the gambler wins. Compare that to one of life's tragedies. But over time, the house, or goodness, wins. That is, we may have too narrow a view of tragedy.

Whatever the case, the sad fact is that science brings us no further along than religion. We are left without an ultimate answer. There is no adequate explanation for creation. Everyone is left believing in some force beyond our understanding.

EXERCISES

I was once walking with one of my daughters when she was about three years old. We were outside in the bright sunshine when a butterfly fluttered by us. My daughter stopped, stared, and told me, "That's the third butterfly I've ever seen in my life." I can recall wonderful experiences with nature especially, such as standing in front of the ocean in winter and feeling the power of the waves coming at me, filling me with a sense of power or standing with my father one evening in the White Mountains in New Hampshire as a blood-red sun sat seemingly right in front of us.

So seek to connect in your own way. Look for the most beautiful place near you and visit it. Stand outside at night and watch the sky telling you its story of the evening. Stand in the empire of the velvet darkness and feel part of it.

Consider all the options about understanding natural evil. Is there no God? Is there the traditional God who is all-powerful and all-good and therefore responsible for natural evil but whose ways we don't understand? Did God create the natural world in a way that would inevitably lead to life but which isn't controlled?

Can you accept the idea that there are no miracles, that God can't interfere? I had a friend who used to pray that the traffic lights would stay green. I sometimes offered the view to him that perhaps God should more rightly focus on saving babies, but my friend kept praying. I understand his impulses, and I understand why it is so difficult to let go of a protecting God.

4

THE ORIGIN OF HUMAN BEINGS

She lived about two hundred thousand years ago, probably in East Africa because that is where *Homo sapiens sapiens* (those with a modern human anatomy) appeared. All humans who are alive today descend from her through their mother, their mother's mother, and so on through each mother going back to her.

Of course, she is affectionately known as Eve (or, more technically, Mitochrondrial Eve) and she is the most recent of our common matrilineal ancestors. And there was a comparable male, known as Y-chromosomal Adam, the most recent common ancestor from fathers. This Adam and Eve weren't romantically involved though; Adam lived thousands of years separately from Eve.

THE TRADITIONAL ACCOUNT OF CREATION

Human genetics does not provide as poetic or simple a story as the biblical tale of Adam and Eve. And the Bible account has a deliberate moral dimension that science does not include.

According to Jewish tradition, God created Adam and Eve, making it therefore clear that all humans were ultimately created by God. That is, all humans have an equal spiritual relationship with God. And, as the story of Adam and Eve in Genesis makes clear, all humans descend from a single couple. This means that all humans are ultimately related, part of a single universal family.

Such a focus on the creation of a single man and then one couple that created all humans provided support for the theological idea of one God. As the Talmud notes: "He created in the beginning one man only so that heretics should not say that there are several Powers in heaven." A similar conclusion was drawn from the case that Adam and Eve weren't created together because if they had been created together it might have been concluded that there were two gods. If more than one couple had been created, there would have been claims that good people came from one couple and bad people from another. With a single common mother and father, people can't boast that their ancestors are better than another person's. It is compelling that in the sacred literature of the Jewish people, God creates humans before the specific particular existence of the Jewish people.

The creation through a single couple not only provides a shared human origin and a shared family connection but also includes the idea of a shared history and fate, a shared destiny and a shared potential for redemption, a rescue from the human condition.

Because all humans are connected, God is concerned about humanity's collective fate and therefore the course of human history. Such a history includes within it the hope that a common background and a common recognition of God can unite people. Indeed, the single universal family means people have an implied duty to each other combined with a common purpose to act for the good of all people. On this reading, the division of people needs on this interpretation to be ended and humanity's unity restored.

The division had its own purpose. Unity's end spread humans throughout the world according to God's plan to fill the world, to have diversity because moral needs are varied, and diverse people will have diverse skills, which, performed as in an orchestra, produces a unified and pleasing result.

According to Jewish tradition, humans were created in God's image (e.g., Genesis 1:25–26). It is important to recall that later, at Mount Sinai, God purportedly commanded that no idol depicting God be made. God was not, on this principle, to take human shape; first, because God was not human; second, because no human should be worshipped as God; and third, because the absence of a visual God reminded humans of their own spiritual vocation. Human beings have intellectual abilities, the capacity to commune with God, to be partners with God, to be in common effort with God for moral activities.

The fact that humans are made in God's image has its own moral implications. If we harm another person, we are in some sense harming God—hence the biblical injunction to "love your neighbor as yourself" (Leviticus 19:18). Nevertheless, as the Talmud points out, humans, unlike God, have a body that is earthly and are therefore doomed one day to die.

To the Rabbis of the Talmud, it was clear that the purpose of earthly existence was to glorify God, to follow the Torah and the mitzvot, because when they die they are "exempt from Torah and the commandments, and the Holy One, blessed be He, can derive no praise from him." Therefore, the acquisition of goods was of no lasting value. Rather, the point of life was to acquire moral actions. The goal of life is not to be happy; it is to be good. The treasure of collected moral behaviors, the Rabbis asserted, had value that transcended death. "In the hour of man's departure neither silver nor gold nor precious stones nor pearls accompany him, but only Torah and good works."

THE THEORY OF EVOLUTION

The account of the creation of human beings in classical Jewish literature is not meant to be a chapter in a scientific textbook. For that reason, while other religions may have struggled with the Darwinian theory of natural selection, Jews generally accepted it as compatible with their religion. Reform, Conservative, Reconstructionist, and Modern Orthodox Jews do not question Darwin, or the evidence of the age of the Earth, or other comparable scientific evidence. Many religious people assert that Genesis is not a science account but God's plan for humans expressed in vivid, poetic imagery.

However, sometimes this acceptance is misleading because it implies a compromise that Darwin didn't make. It is not the case that natural selection is just a way that God used to shape the course of evolution so that, inevitably, human beings would emerge. However comforting for theists, including Jews, such an apparent compromise between science and religion might be, natural selection in fact has deeply disturbing consequences for traditional religious thought. Natural selection, by which organisms that are better adapted to their environment tend to survive and produce more offspring than organisms that are not as well adapted, explains evolutionary changes without invoking any divine purpose at all. Natural selection occurs through an entirely random process of variations. The survivors, those with the best adaptive skills, carry on their particular traits.

Does such a naturalistic understanding of humans leave any room for those who want to accept both a supernatural God and natural selection?

As noted in the discussion of the physics of the creation of the cosmos, a contemporary interpretation of Judaism starts off with the idea that God created the laws that made the world and applies that idea to human beings. In the case of people, God wanted to create intelligent beings with a moral sense and an ability to have an encounter with God. The notion of natural selection had to appear from somewhere. It may make common sense that the surviving organisms are the best at adapting, but why should it be that way? Why couldn't it have been that no organisms survived or changed even if they were good at adaptation? That is, we are in a quandary. Perhaps the laws that govern evolution developed naturally or spontaneously, but it is also at least conceivable that a supernatural God created the algorithm, the set of rules, of natural selection. It should be noted that for theists, such an approach allows for full compatibility with natural selection but limits the role God played in the creation of human beings.

As it did in quantum mechanics, chance played a great role in the creation of human beings. But it is scientifically plausible that such an approach would yield creatures very much like humans in the sense of having intelligence and linguistic skills, and a moral sense that evolved because of the need for reciprocal altruism. On this interpretation evolution discovered these moral skills rather than created them, and the point of creation is the struggle toward what is good. It is also the case, troubling to some, that one implication is that humans didn't have to look exactly as they do. It is obvious, for example, that our bodies have many physical problems, that if God designed our bodies, rather than their being the result of a random evolutionary process, then God could not be considered a very competent engineer. To take one simple example, our retina is backward. Surely if God did the designing, that wouldn't have happened.

In a way, Darwin gives moral cover to God. We don't know every detail of evolution, but if it is done by random natural selection, God is not responsible for how our bodies look, only that we exist and have a mind that seeks the good and can communicate with God.

Nontheists often object to the effort to claim that an interpretation with a moral, supernatural God is equal to a straightforward natural explanation. Such nontheists sometimes claim that there is no need for God in the explanation by the application of Occam's razor, the principle that when there are competing hypotheses to explain the same phenomenon, it makes sense to choose the hypothesis that has the fewest assumptions.

But such an approach ignores the problem of the origins of the laws of evolution. Their existence requires either some meta-evolutionary theory that is natural or a supernatural theory such as God. Occam's razor is equal in both cases.

Additionally, for all that science is capable of answering, it can't answer the simple questions humans have. For example, at the beginning of his book *The Myth of Sisyphus*, the philosopher Albert Camus makes the startling statement that the only important philosophical question is whether or not to commit suicide. Science can't determine whether or not it is worthwhile to live, and yet that is a crucial question in life. Science doesn't even consider such a question. So religion is not superfluous. (It should be noted that in his essay "Return to Tipasa" Camus also wrote: "In the depths of winter, I finally learned that within me there lay an invincible summer.")

All this doesn't prove God created the laws of evolution that led to human beings, but science doesn't disprove the possibility of that God existing.

Nontheists can also turn to the crucial question of the human brain, identical for some naturalists with the idea of mind. For them, our minds developed through evolution so we could adapt to a natural world that is, in the words of Thomas Hobbes, "solitary, poor, nasty, brutish, and short." He might have added "unpredictable."

For many evolutionary psychologists the idea of God evolved as we looked at this world and saw in its workings an intention that was not necessarily there. We might, that is, have over-interpreted what we perceived as intentionality. We saw rain and thought a divine power created it intending to grow crops.

Neurotheology is a relatively new field in which scientists attempt to reduce spiritual experiences to neural phenomena. Neuroscientists, for example, can see images that show specific brain activity during such human practices as meditating about God. The problem with this approach is that such activity does not clarify whether or not there is genuine communication with God. If my brain seems to register that I perceive a large object in a room, that doesn't prove that there is or is not such an object, only that I perceive it.

FREE WILL

Another brain question that is emerging involves free will and determinism. Again, science provides uncomfortable facts for believers.

Much of the Jewish perception of humans seems to revolve around the notion of free will. In the Bible, human history really begins with the free choice of Eve and Adam to eat the fruit from the tree of the knowledge of good and evil.

For traditional Jews, humans have a soul and free will is part of that soul—a crucial part, for humans are, under normal circumstances, capable of discerning between right and wrong and responsible for their actions. Indeed, in a way the making of moral choices defines the Jewish task in life. In Judaism, there is a satisfaction in moral achievement done through our own efforts and by our own will. Without responsibility, there is no meaning to the idea of reward and punishment for one's acts. If we are not responsible for what we do, how can we truly be held morally guilty of the act and punished for it? Therefore, if human responsibility for human actions is removed, Judaism is deeply undermined. As the Talmud notes, "All is in the hands of Heaven except the fear of Heaven."

The Rabbis did not believe in Original Sin, the notion that Adam's sin of disobeying God was passed on to all future generations making everyone sinful even at birth. Rather, the Jewish view is that humans are not born either good or bad. A human's soul at birth is completely innocent and untainted by sin.

Instead of Original Sin, the Rabbis distinguished between a human being's "good inclination" (*yetzer ha-tov*) in conflict with the so-called evil inclination (*yetzer hara*). This doctrine is more complex than it appears to be. Rather than a choice humans must make between good and evil, it is crucial to note that, for the Rabbis, God created all, including the yetzer hara. The evil inclination is not some devilish force within us that drives us to commit a sin, to separate ourselves from God's will or what we take to be a human agreement with God about how to act morally. It is instead a normal human drive that is not used correctly. Suppose we are hungry. That is a normal human drive. But if we steal food we don't need, we have not used the drive God gave us correctly. We have not acted as part of a community but out of selfish needs. Or we could eat food we legally obtain but eat too much of it. Such gluttonous behavior injures the holy bodies that we need to use in the service of God and ourselves. Humans, according to the Rabbis, have the free choice to decide which inclination they will choose. As Moshe Chaim Luzzato (1707–1746) wrote in *The Way of God*, "Man is the creature created for the purpose of being drawn close to God. He is placed between perfection and deficiency, with the power to earn perfection. Man must earn this perfection, however, through his own free will. . . . Man's inclinations are therefore balanced between good . . . and evil . . . and he is not compelled toward either of them. He has the power of choice and is able to choose either side knowingly and willingly."

There were Jewish groups that denied free will. The Essenes were a sect of Jews who were most popular from about the second century BCE to the first century CE. They lived communally and practiced an ascetic existence avoiding worldly activities. They were mystics who believed they were living as the world was ending. Some scholars ascribe the Dead Sea Scrolls to the Essenes. The Essenes believed in predestination, with God predetermining all that happened. The Sadducees, a larger sect that lived in Judea in that era, consisted of the upper social class of the time. They believed events occurred by chance.

But these were not normative views. Much of Jewish law rests on an understanding that humans have moral and legal responsibility even though it is clear that sometimes there are imposed limits on our freedom that we can't control, such as when we are compelled to act incorrectly.

Talmudic Rabbis strolled with a seeming contradiction. If God has foreknowledge of our actions, as the Rabbis believed, how could humans choose freely? The Rabbis accepted human freedom as well and refrained from offering a definitive solution to the quandary of how both could be true. They claimed that "everything is foreseen yet permission [human freedom] is given."

Free will, as understood by classical Judaism, was a powerful weapon for people. For each time they made a decision they changed their lives and the world, remaking it in a new way. They were, in a sense, acting as though they were truly made in God's image, for they were, through their free actions, constantly re-creating the world they inhabited. The freely made decisions over time constructed a self and defined a personality. Those decisions reflected a person's character, even as it was being constructed. It was this free ability to make choices that made people fully human.

Maimonides (*Yad. Teshuva* 5:3) asserts that free will is "a great principle and pillar of the Torah and mitzvot." He thought the kind of knowledge God had was different from human knowledge. God, he believed, is living in an eternal present because God is outside the time that humans must live through. God can therefore see, while humans have free will.

Free will allows for self-reflection and self-correction. The whole idea of repentance is, for example, at the heart of the Yom Kippur service. To repent presumes that humans have the free will to repent. God, on this account, will forgive if humans can freely choose to recognize the errors of their past and free themselves from sin so they may walk with God.

Attending services at Yom Kippur has affected many lives. Franz Rosenzweig (1886–1929) was arguably the most influential Jewish theologian of the twentieth century. His early philosophy evolved into an existential outlook, focusing on the individual experiences of people, and probing how religion shaped an individual's experience. He saw a person's relationship with God as an encounter. Oddly enough, his interest in religion was aroused by his close friend Eugen Rosenstock-Huessy, who had become a Protestant and who convinced Rosenzweig that a scholar could, with intellectual justification, also be religious.

The two friends talked through most of the night of July 7, 1913. Seeking a breakthrough, Rosenzweig asked his friend how to find answers. Rosenstock-Huessy gave the simplest of religious responses; he urged Rosenzweig to pray. Rosenzweig didn't pray. Instead he reached a conclusion that he, too, would embrace Christianity, because it was acceptable to his friend and some members of his own family.

Having made his fateful decision, Rosenzweig concluded that he should enter Christianity not as a pagan but, as the religion's founder had, as a Jew. The logic drove him to attend Rosh Hashanah and Yom Kippur services to pass through Judaism to Christianity.

It was with such a plan in mind that he was sitting in an Orthodox synagogue in Berlin on Yom Kippur, October 11, 1913. He spent the entire day listening to the services, listening in the evening to the Kol Nidre declaration and the next day to the psalms and hymns, the scriptural readings, and the rest of the emotionally overwhelming service. He heard the story of Jonah—the tale of a prophet who tried to flee from the service of God. Surely, Rosenzweig's mind found resonance in such a story. The service ended with the congregational professions of the faith and the sounding of the ram's horn.

Rosenzweig left the services as a transformed man. The day made him realize he could find meaning within Judaism. It is not necessary to leave it. He wrote a long letter to his mother, trying to explain what had happened.

It was at the end of August 1918 that he began his most famous work, *The Star of Redemption*. He was a soldier at the time, and he wrote what he could on military postcards that he sent home to his mother. It was only when the war ended that he returned to finish one of the most important books in Jewish theology.

Traditional Judaism saw Rosenzweig's spiritual experience as an encounter with God by a free human being, not a neurological accident.

Neuroscience has made some discoveries that, like other scientific discoveries at other times, upset our commonsense notion of the cosmos and human beings. For example, it seems clear now that the brain has already made decisions before we are consciously aware of those decisions. We are shaped by unconscious processes of which we are not aware, by our backgrounds and so on, in ways our conscious mind does not recognize. In this sense, it does appear that free will is illusory. But, despite this, we are still responsible for what we do. Responsibility, on this account, is a social concept not a brain concept, and we are responsible for following the rules of society. Such an approach has its own weaknesses. Were Nazis acting with responsibility by following the rules of Nazi society? Didn't they have the moral responsibility to rebel against the genocidal intentions of their leaders?

But if by a society, we mean a religious community, an inherited moral system, then we can frame the question differently. We have many unconscious, often emotional, processes shaping our thoughts and desires, but these are tempered by, for example, the moral guidance provided by the Jewish tradition. Consider Adam and Eve in the Garden of Eden, tempted by the serpent and filled with unconscious processes that prompted their conscious minds to think that they wanted to eat the fruit. But God's command, then the only religious guidance available, was that they not eat the fruit. Despite their possible lack of free will, they still, because of that guidance, were responsible for the choice to follow the promptings of their mind rather than the religious teaching. The implications of this for human beings are twofold. First of all, it is important to study religious ethics to understand how to behave. But this by itself is inadequate if the religious ethics we study lead us astray in such ways as coming to believe that it is God's will that we kill innocent people in God's name. Therefore, prior to studying religious ethics, it is crucial to find such a religious ethical system that emphasizes human freedom, recognizes the value of human life, and provides examples of exemplary moral behavior. We are free to study religious and secular moral systems that do this. Obviously, for example, this book operates under the assumption that Jewish moral beliefs provide good guidance for human behavior.

Our deepest moral responsibility, then, is to choose a moral system to follow that provides the most moral of outcomes, restricts our freedom to act morally the least, and provides the most coherent justification of its precepts. This sounds good, but there is an infinite regression to such a view. Were the people who developed the moral system free to make their choices, or did their brains and circumstances force them to make such decisions? And so on and on until it is not clear that humans are free to make such choices of moral systems because the origins of the systems are always suspect.

There is a way out of this dilemma. And only one way. Without choosing this way, human responsibility remains suspect. That way is that God is the revealer of the moral system. The nature and mechanisms of such revelations will be dealt with in a later chapter. At this point it is sufficient to note that without accepting that a moral system ultimately derives from God, there is no system of human responsibility that can be defended from the views of the strict determinist. If we accept the notion of revelation, then our moral responsibility rests on understanding and responding to the revelation from God.

Contemporary Jews who wish to retain theism, in this sense, have an advantage if they wish also to retain a belief in humans being responsible for their actions.

For those who believe in God's revelation, it should be noted that there was a revelation given beyond the Torah that was meant for all humanity. These are known as the Noahide Laws, the moral code meant for the "children of Noah," consisting of all humanity. By tradition, the first six of the laws (listed, for example, in the Talmud, in Sanhedin 56a) were given to Adam before he was forced to leave the Garden of Eden. The seventh law was added after the Flood. The Seven Laws that righteous Gentiles should follow include:

1. Prohibiting idolatry
2. Prohibiting murder
3. Prohibiting theft
4. Prohibiting sexual misconduct
5. Prohibiting blasphemy
6. Prohibiting eating a living animal's flesh
7. Establishing law courts

But why should humans obey these laws? Humans have many struggles with their lives including those as they try to understand God and God's laws. No struggle is bigger than trying to understand evil.

EXERCISES

Jewish law includes the notion that the human body is holy because it encases the soul. Therefore, there are various commandments to take care of the body. For example, mutilating the body is forbidden (Leviticus 19:27–28; Deuteronomy 23:3). What is your religious attitude toward the body? In what ways do you treat it as sacred and in what ways don't you?

There are Jewish prayers for the sick and prayers for good health. The Mi Shebeirach prayer, for example, includes these words: "Bless those in need of healing with the renewal of body, the renewal of spirit, and let us say amen." The Hasidic master Nachman of Breslov (1772–1810) believed that ten of the Psalms had special powers to do healing. These are Psalms 16, 32, 41, 42, 59, 77, 90, 105, 137, and 150. Read Psalm 77

as an example of these. Create your own prayer for a longing
to be healed. Meditate about the place of your body as part of
your whole being.

Both by the biblical and scientific account, we all come from
the same ancestor, Eve. What does it mean, both in a literal and
figurative sense, to have a common ancestor?

What are your beliefs about free will? Are you really responsible for your actions? What would it mean if people weren't
responsible?

(5)

THE SUFFERING
OF THE INNOCENT

THE TRADITIONAL JEWISH EXPLANATION
OF GOOD AND EVIL

According to the Bible, God is "the shaper of light and creator of darkness, the maker of well-being and creator of evil" (Isaiah 45:7). There is no biblical attempt to claim that another cosmic force created evil, no Devil equal in power to God. That God created evil, however, does not imply that God doesn't care about evil in human lives or that evil is central to God's essential nature. If God is good, though, it seems logical that the Bible would discuss why God created evil, but it doesn't. Evil in the Bible is just a brutal fact of life; there is no philosophical inquiry as to its reasons.

Perhaps that is why Rabbi Harold Kushner didn't title his famous 1978 book on the subject *Why Bad Things Happen to Good People* but rather *When Bad Things Happen to Good People.* Knowing suffering is inevitable, Rabbi Kushner, like the Bible, is interested in how humans react when suffering and pain overwhelm them and reality seems to mock fairness,

justice, and reason. He is interested in how people should react to terrible events, how to recover from the tragic. Kushner
doesn't think there is an adequate answer to the question of
why people suffer.

Rabbi Kushner's book originated after his family's experiences with their young son, Aaron, who suffered from progeria.
Children who have progeria have symptoms that make them
appear to age, so they look like the elderly at a young age. They
typically die at some point from their mid-teens to early twen-
ties. In Aaron's case, he died in 1977 at the age of fourteen. It
is easy to imagine a family that went through this experience
angrily abandoning all faith in a good, all-powerful, all-knowing
God. Rabbi Kushner's book is an attempt to help those who
have suffered some evil walk their way through the depths of
the emotional valley in which they can find themselves. It is an
attempt to hold on to some notion of God while facing the depth
and scope of the suffering.

The word *theodicy*, coined by Gottfried Leibnitz, is the attempt to reconcile God's goodness and the evil we experience.
All efforts at theodicy have found success elusive.

The Bible sees the struggle between good and evil and envi-
sions God struggling along with humans. But the biblical answer
to human suffering is blunt: evil happens as a consequence of
our actions. "No harm befalls the righteous, but the wicked are
full of misfortune" (Proverbs 12:21). Humans were, on the biblical account, given the freedom to do good or not, and sometimes they choose to do evil. When they do, they suffer.

Why did God even allow a choice? Why not design humans
so they had to choose the good? That would make a much more
satisfying world, and reduce the suffering that resulted from
sin. But the possibility of moral growth was so crucial to God's
purpose that evil was allowed, because without it humans would

have no choice but to be good. They would not be free beings. They could not grow morally.

The Book of Job is the most important biblical work about human suffering. It differs from the more common biblical notion of suffering as Godly retribution for human sin in offering other answers instead. The book is about Job, a good man, and a successful one, with three daughters and seven sons. Job is faithful to God, a model example of the sort of person who does not deserve to suffer. A character known as "The Satan" appears. Note that "Satan" is not a name but perhaps a reference to a job like a prosecutor in a court of law. The Satan's powers ultimately derive from God. God asks the Satan about Job. The Satan, being a prosecutor, argues that Job is certainly righteous but only because he has been prosperous and blessed. The Satan presses the case by claiming that if God took all that Job had away, then Job would no longer be righteous or praise God. In response, God gave The Satan permission to act, and so Job loses his oxen, donkeys, sheep, and camels. Then Job's ten children are killed. Job continues to accept what he believes to be God's judgment and does not curse God. Allowed to afflict Job personally, but not to kill him, The Satan gives him boils. Job's wife tells him to curse God, but he does not. Three of Job's friends arrive, supposedly to console him for all the horror that has befallen him. A fourth friend also is there. They argue that Job's suffering is, like all suffering, a punishment for sin. Job rebels against such an idea, asserting his innocence from sin. That is, the Book of Job is a repudiation of the idea that suffering is a punishment for sin.

But then Job must ask, if he has not sinned, why has God chosen to punish him? Job considers a possible reward in the afterlife. He ponders the possibility that God is simply testing him. But there, in the middle of the pain, he cannot find solace in these answers. It is then that Job hears God's voice. God notes that Job is indeed righteous, but asserts that Job cannot truly understand the ways of God. Therefore, humans like Job must confess that humans have only limited knowledge and that God and God's ways cannot truly be known. The world is moral, but, according to the Book of Job, we cannot understand how that morality works.

Job's health is restored. He has a new family and a new appreciation of the human condition, one in which suffering remains a painful mystery.

For the Rabbis in the Talmudic era, the Book of Job theme of the certainty of a just fate in the afterlife rendered earthly injustice more acceptable and sensible. As Rabbi Akiva put it, God is "exact with the righteous, holding them to account for the few wrongs they committed in this world, in order to lavish bliss upon them and give them a goodly reward in the world-to-come. . . . [God] lavishes ease upon the wicked and rewards them in this world for the few good deeds they performed in order to retaliate against them in the world-to-come."

In his famous medieval work *The Guide for the Perplexed*, Maimonides distinguishes between natural evil and two kinds of human evil, evil like murder that is caused by other people and evil that humans bring on themselves.

At the beginning of the modern era, Hermann Cohen reaffirmed the idea that the Jewish people were God's "suffering servant," and through their suffering offered a challenge to others to be ethical, a constant poke at humanity's conscience.

None of these ideas served to answer the question of suffering. If, to take a dramatic example, God hears a child crying because of a cruel adult and doesn't care, then God is not all-good. If God doesn't hear the child cry or hears the cry and can't fix the problem, then God is not all-powerful.

Rabbi Kushner finds the answer that makes the most sense to him in the final response. God's power is limited. This limit is not by choice. God is not in control of the cosmos. That is why bad things happen.

Rabbi Kushner took his idea from Rabbi Mordecai Kaplan, the founder of Reconstructionism, who said God's limitations were built into God. It should be noted that Kaplan's idea of God was not traditional. For him, God was not a supernatural being but the natural forces that battle evil.

This response is different from Jewish tradition in that neither Kaplan nor Kushner believes that God is responsible for the suffering of the innocent. Kaplan, though, represents the optimism of the era in which he grew up. He thinks the power in nature that fights evil will inevitably triumph. Kushner is more pessimistic. He seems to suggest that evil isn't going anywhere, and we will have to learn that nature is unavoidably going to lead to suffering for all of us in varying degrees.

For many contemporary Jews, the Holocaust represents the greatest impediment to understanding God. Anyone, for example, who has been to the Children's Memorial at Yad Vashem in Jerusalem is confronted by the unknowable and unanswerable question of evil. The Children's Memorial was hollowed out of an underground cavern. It exists as a tribute to the million and a half Jewish children who were victims of the Holocaust. The memorial's candles seem to reflect infinitely in the darkness giving the appearance of an endless expanse of stars in the sky. The names of the victims, with their ages and countries of origin, accompany the lights. The goodness of God seems lost in that darkness and raises a fundamental question: Why does a good God permit any human suffering at all or any cruelty by people toward others?

For some Jewish theologians, the Holocaust is a continuation of the sort of horrific tragedies that have punctuated different parts of Jewish history. But other thinkers look at the Holocaust and see a novel event, unprecedented even by the catastrophes that the Jewish people experienced earlier in their history. For many Jews, the classical biblical explanation that God sent this punishment because of the sins of the people is impossible to accept in the light of the death of six million innocent Jews. Indeed, all the explanations of evil fail to provide solace or understanding. The anger that flows naturally from an honest look at the Holocaust led some to the loss of faith or to the hatred of God. Such hatred resulted for some who continued to believe in a worship marked by anger and protest. Such a position marked by this disdain for God is called Misotheism.

Responding to the Holocaust has led some Jewish thinkers to radical new understandings. Rabbi Richard Rubenstein famously argued that the Holocaust represents the "death of God," that is, the end of our ability to believe in a good God in the way we had. Rubinstein concludes, "When I say we live in the time of the death of God, I mean that the thread uniting God and Man, heaven and earth, has been broken. We stand in a cold, silent, unfeeling cosmos, unaided by any purposeful power beyond our own resources. After Auschwitz what else can a Jew say about God? . . . The time of the death of God does not mean the end of all gods. It means the demise of the God who was the ultimate actor in history."

This somber vision, realistic as it is, never found a large following within Judaism. Perhaps Rubinstein's language is too blunt, or the metaphorical image of a dead God too emotionally overwhelming. But the theology underneath the provocative language remains important and is discussed below.

Martin Buber's notion of an "eclipse of God" softens Rubinstein's language, but remains unsatisfactory. Why would there be an eclipse of an all-powerful, all-good God? If we understood such an eclipse as a Godly step, necessary so that humans retain their freedom of action, then the Holocaust isn't so much a failure of God as it is a failure of humans. But, as neuroscience is there to remind us, the very notion of human freedom is not as obvious as the Jewish tradition suggests so that this explanation of evil also has its problems. Buber consistently emphasized the importance of relationships with others, and so for him human evil's end begins with the establishing of genuine and caring relationships with other people.

For Abraham Joshua Heschel, God has provided humans with the mitzvot, and these divine commandments provide the mechanism by which humans are able to overcome the evil in their hearts and live by the goodness they possess. Other thinkers such as Eliezer Berkovits have agreed that humans bear responsibility for the Holocaust, not God, for God is a teacher who offered humans moral lessons that humans ignored or flouted. Others saw the Jews as some sort of sacrifice required for ultimate human redemption. Rabbi Emil Fackenheim saw in the Holocaust a crucial call to remain Jewish, for not to do so would be to hand Hitler a "posthumous victory." Other Jewish thinkers reacted to this, saying it is not an answer because denying Hitler was no substitute for affirming Judaism.

And so we are left adrift. In the face of evil, is there a new approach, one that coheres with science, and leaves an ethical God who reveals truths to humans?

CONTEMPORARY JUDAISM AND EVIL

As we have seen, the problem of evil is painfully obvious: no abstract explanation, no moral impulse, no invocation of a kind, wise, and loving God gives us the ability to explain the death of a child or the seemingly endless and needless suffering that sensitive observers confront every day of their lives. Just as we begin to feel, with Kant, "the starry sky above me and the moral law within me" we crash into the world's horrors. Why, we wonder,

are humans capable of willfully inflicting pain on others, sometimes horrifically so and sometimes on a scale so massive that the
depths of human depravity seem to be bottomless? Why do the
good sometimes suffer and the evil sometimes prosper?

It seems obscene, in the face of this intense suffering, to talk
about a good God. There are no emotionally satisfying answers
to evil because none of the answers removes evil. A good, all-
powerful God seemingly has the power to stop evil but seems
unable or unwilling to do so. There are many well-known attempts to explain this horrifying problem, but the history of
theodicy, however subtle and clever and well-meaning, dissolves
with the death of an innocent child or the genocidal intentions
of murderous nations.

For those who accept that God created the cosmos using
natural laws to do so, there is still a gnawing question. Why did
God not create a perfect cosmos? Why is our world so filled
with imperfections? Why does lightning kill an innocent person
seemingly at random? Why are there earthquakes and torna-
does and hurricanes? Surely an all-powerful, all-good God could
have created a universe without these evils of nature?

Of course what are sometimes called natural evils would not
even be considered as aberrations without the regular natural
laws. Chaos would reign without the rhythms of the cosmos.
The very notion of disorder implies an order to which these
events didn't conform or stood outside.

It is possible to assert that the natural world with all its imperfections has what we call disasters for a reason. A perfect world
would have left human beings with no natural entity to improve
and so a natural world incapable of shaping our moral values.
That is, it is at least theoretically possible to see a moral reason
to some disasters.

For instance, consider a world without natural dangers. In
such a place, there would be no need to be concerned about

others getting hurt, no empathy for earthquake victims or a young mother with a brain tumor, fewer chances for humans to be heroic and so reduced opportunities for people to test themselves and to undergo moral growth.

But for most people, the price is way too high for the possibility of a moral lesson. Surely, a Being as clever as God could have come up with a way to impart moral lessons without triggering them through the unmerited and random suffering that often accompanies natural disasters.

There are other explanations, including the simple notion that God's ways are inscrutable to us, that we see only a tiny dot of the cosmos and cannot see it all the way God does.

However accurate the central point, this approach remains unsatisfying on several levels. Why would God create us and make us unable to comprehend our lives? And why wouldn't a good God provide more clarity?

Of course, as many atheists assert, the alternative to all this is that we don't understand God because there is no God to understand. God didn't create the universe.

But what if we accept science and still believe in God as a transcendent Being who provides meaning and purpose to human existence? Can we find a middle ground, a way to explain natural evil in some other way?

We can invoke the idea of a fine-tuned universe to argue that the natural world had to be the particular physical and mathematical structure it is to allow intelligent beings capable of apprehending God, being moral, and being partners with God. That is, God didn't want to create angels, but humans, and the only path to doing that was to create laws that would eventually lead to a specific type of being: humans. But using a material reality to create the sort of beings who were spiritually fully free to believe or not, to question or not, to achieve or not, to be partners with God or not required certain materials. Creating material reality at all placed limits on God, but using a material reality that would lead to life and ultimately to moral humans placed severe limits. On this interpretation, the material reality that is the cosmos is the best physically consistent universe possible if the goal is to create beings such as we are with our minds. Maybe Leibnitz's view that this is the best of all possible worlds, a view mocked by Voltaire in *Candide*, turns out to be more subtle and accurate than expected.

This approach does not satisfy all physicists but it does some prominent ones, including John Barrow and Freeman Dyson. Theists may breathe a sigh of relief, but they shouldn't. An understanding of a God who created such a cosmos with all those limitations coheres with evolution and neuroscience, but carries with it unnerving implications.

On this interpretation, having set up the materials and laws of the cosmos to produce moral human beings, God evidently could not then interfere physically with the ongoing creation. To do so would disrupt the very laws that let it operate, and in so doing disrupt its structure and purpose. Perhaps, for example, a disruption would alter the moral nature of humans. Therefore in this view God cannot stop natural evil.

With such an approach, contemporary theists have a theory that is fully compatible with science but no longer have the traditional Jewish idea of an all-powerful, good God permitting evil. Indeed, instead, such believers have a morally powerful God—wanting to improve the moral state of the world, seeking out human partners to do so, and providing revelations for those who listen—but one who is not responsible for natural evil, does not sympathize with the human condition, and will not offer moral guidance and solace even as we suffer.

One consequence of seeing God as not being all-powerful is that we can come to see other figures of power (the president, our doctor, our professors, and others) in a new way. They are not all-powerful either. We will come to have diminished expectations of their ability to protect us and guide our lives. The only positive side of this is that we will need to take more responsibility. We are in charge of our health, not our doctors. We are in charge of our education, not our teachers. It is a tougher life to live if we see the implications of diminished powers of the authorities we accept.

God can communicate with humans, not through miracles, but through the mysterious process of revelation, through a personal encounter. This process is unclear. Some theists argue for a propositional content to this encounter in which God communicates directly with the minds of individual humans. Others believe that there is no propositional encounter, that in some inexpressible manner, God inspires humans, who then put the inspiration into words. The formulation of the purported revelation, either directly or by inspiration, can then be passed on and influence other people and even history. The Bible is, of course, the most significant example of this.

This notion of revelation is crucial because through it a nonphysical God can influence physical humans who can act in the world. Therefore the idea that God cannot intervene in the world is more complex than it seems. If God cannot interrupt history to correct a wrong, that does not imply that God can't try to influence people by revelation to correct the wrong.

One way to look at this is that God, being unable to act, needs humans to act as moral agents. The partnership between God and human is therefore a moral one.

We may have to give up the comforting idea that God protects us. If we see God as not being able to interfere in the natural world, then God can't save us when we get sick. There are no natural miracles.

But even the idea of miracles is complex. Note that, unlike Kaplan for example, the God described here is supernatural, concerned about humans, and able to communicate with humans. So if I'm undergoing an operation, it is not reasonable to pray to God to heal me, but it is reasonable to pray to God to communicate with the doctors who will operate on me, to inspire them, to give them insights if they are able and willing to hear and respond to God's revelations. God is not powerless, but the powers are of a special kind.

Of course, in giving up this comfort we also get a lot. God can provide comfort by providing inspiration when we're in trouble. We can retain a moral companionship with God. And we don't have to deal with the painful dilemma of God permitting evil.

That is a deal worth considering, but it is not a great deal.

The God that such an interpretation of contemporary Judaism yields is neither emotionally satisfying nor the Being we traditionally understand as God. It is for these reasons that evil is the great mystery it is. We are each left with two principal choices: (1) a kind, loving, all-powerful God permits the evil in the world and we have to accept that without understanding it; or (2) God is not all-powerful and cannot interfere with the world. That leaves God as not responsible for evil in the world, and therefore as purely good and a suitable moral partner, but this God is not the God of tradition or a God who satisfies our profound emotional need to have a protector. Ultimately, God is responsible for the evil, of course, but that was an inevitable companion to human existence. God's choice, then, was either no evil or no humans.

DOUBT

It is no wonder, then, that human beings doubt the existence of God or the goodness of God or the fairness of God in allowing the scope and intensity of human suffering.

Given the complexity of evil, it even seems unreasonable to avoid doubt. Doubting God is not the same as denying God. In Judaism it is not a sin to doubt. Neither is doubt the creation of some dark urge that challenges God. After all, if we believe everything or if we doubt everything, we have found a sure path to avoid thinking. Doubt is not the opposite of faith. Henry David Thoreau put it well, "Faith keeps many doubts in her pay. If I could not doubt, I should not believe."

All this is why a good believer has some doubt and a good doubter has some belief. Elie Wiesel, the Holocaust survivor, author of the memoir *Night*, and winner of the Nobel Peace Prize, suggests that after the death of so many Jews, we are all entitled to ask God six million questions. The human task, he suggests, is not to understand God but to question.

Wiesel did so in a 1979 play titled *The Trial of God (as it was held on February 25, 1649, in Shamgorod)*. The play is fictitious, with God called as the defendant in a Jewish court for remaining silent as many innocent Jews were murdered. As a teenager in Auschwitz, Wiesel witnessed three inmates holding such a trial. Wiesel's play, however, is not set in a concentration camp but in 1649 in a Ukrainian village in the aftermath of pogroms that resulted in the death of almost all the Jews who lived there. God is ultimately found innocent after a stranger defends the Almighty; the stranger is The Satan as depicted in Job.

There was also a television play titled *God on Trial*. The play, fictional like Wiesel's, was written by Frank Cottrell Boye. It is set in a concentration camp with passionate arguments against God. The three inmates conducting the trial find God guilty, but allow that there are grounds for God to appeal the verdict.

There is a tale about the Hasidic Rabbi Levi Yitzhak of Berditchev that on one Rosh Hashanah the rabbi issued a challenge to God to appear in a lawsuit for keeping the Jews suffering in exile.

It should be noted that arguing with God is a Jewish tradition. Those who engaged in such arguments include biblical prophets like Jeremiah, who questioned God's justice and fairness to him. The idea, as Wiesel so movingly illustrates, is that it is the very act of questioning, of doubting, or arguing that brings Jews closer to God. The relationship is more intimate, more equal, not in the sense of power but in the sense of moral partnership. The arguments with God are family arguments. To remain silent would indicate that God cannot be approached or that God is indifferent to human suffering. The point of such efforts is that while we cannot live without questioning, for many Jews we also cannot live without God. Indeed, the original trial in Auschwitz ended with the men conducting the trial dispersing for afternoon prayers. The trial, for them, was a legitimate part of Judaism's religious outlook.

But many Jews believe they can live without God. Can a person be Jewish and an atheist? The simple answer is yes, because any person born of a Jewish mother or who has converted to Judaism is Jewish. (There are numerous internal disputes about conversion, including who can perform a conversion and the requirements for conversion.) Beyond that, because Judaism has no required belief system, there is no requirement for a belief in God. According to Jewish law, however, a person must still obey the commandments. For modern secular Jews, who identify as Jewish because of culture, temperament, traditions, and other factors independent of any religious affiliation, the issue is more complicated, and, as for everyone, each atheist Jew must work out what is believed and what isn't. It should be pointed out, though, that the struggling with belief, the thinking through of what is accepted and what is not, is a form of belief. Such a Jew who spiritually wrestles with the Jewish tradition is different from the indifferent Jew who doesn't care enough to struggle.

Most American Jews, whatever their doubts and struggles, are not ready to deny God's presence, even if the lives they lead are filled with questions.

EXERCISES

Can you find enough comfort in a God who cannot interfere in the natural world except through trying to communicate comfort and morality to humans? If not, can you accept a God who has the power to change the world and yet allows an uneven allocation of justice and suffering?

With a few friends, hold a trial with God as the defendant for allowing evil in the world. Someone should be chosen to accuse God, someone to defend God, and the others to serve as the jury.

Imagine you are God. (Congratulations on the promotion.) How would you change the world? Think of the good and bad effects of that change.

6

THE JEWISH PEOPLE

Albert Einstein once startled an audience. He was widely known as the most intelligent human alive, the man who had escaped and enraged the Nazis, and the man who had coaxed deeply held secrets out of a reluctant natural world. But the audience wasn't ready for what he was about to say. He interrupted his own lecture and suddenly announced, "I'm sorry I was born a Jew." The members of the audience were shocked into a hush. How could this great man make such an outlandish statement? Einstein then impishly continued, "Because it deprived me of the privilege of choosing to be a Jew."

Many great people were similarly deprived of that privilege because, like Einstein, they, too, had been born Jewish. Moses. King David. Queen Esther. Freud. Golda Meir. The Marx Brothers. Or more contemporary people such as Bob Dylan, Jon Stewart, Natalie Portman, and so many others. It would take a book just to list the Jews who have made a crucial contribution to culture or politics or science or some other field. That includes many inventions by Jews that are not widely known, such as the microphone (Emile Berliner), the hot dog bun (Abraham Levis), and the traffic light (Charles Adler). And yet the Jews have always been and remain a miniscule percentage of the human population. Jews are justly proud of those among their people who have written great books, or discovered a cure for a terrible disease, or taught in schools, or helped the poor and hungry. Beyond pride, though, it is a crucial question to ask where the Jews came from. This is not a history book, however. Instead here there is a focus on a spiritual answer to that question.

In the charting of basic Jewish beliefs, it logically follows that after God created the world and human beings, the next step was to provide humans with moral guidance. Humans already did have their reasoning abilities. They did experience natural laws, the flow of history, and relationships with other human beings. But evidently God wanted to express a morality that transcended the natural world by revealing a specifically spiritual set of moral teachings. According to Jewish tradition, God chose to do this through designating moral messengers, and chose one particular people, the Jews, to be those messengers.

ELECTION: THE CHOSEN PEOPLE

For Jews, then, the election, or choice, of the Jewish people refers to the belief that God revealed the Torah, a way of living often translated as law, that would be the foundation of a nation. God also chose to reveal a morality that was meant for all humanity to one specific group of people. In Exodus 19:5 God calls the Israelites "my treasured possession among all the peoples." The harmonious relationship implied between God and this small people had a crucial historical effect. It made the Jews see themselves as a people apart, a separate people with what would later emerge as special Godly tasks: "You shall be to me a kingdom of priests and a holy nation" (Exodus 19:6).

The most obvious question for those who try to comprehend the meaning of the chosen people is why God chose to convey a message only to some people rather than all people at once. The answer to this is, in part, that God chose to have spiritual teachers available to all humanity, not that God had intense concern for one group of people and limited concern for the remainder of humanity. This is not just an excuse made to cover up any Jewish view that God favored the Jews. Such favoritism would have been seen with God creating Jews as the first people or starting the Jewish calendar with the creation of Jews. But the Bible begins with Adam, the metaphorical ancestor of all humanity, not Abraham, the first Jew. And the Jewish calendar begins with the creation of the world, not the birth of the Jewish people.

It is also important to note that if Jews saw themselves as innately superior, the religion would never have legally allowed converts to enter the Jewish faith and would not have actively sought converts as Jews did at various times in their history. Judaism, that is, is not exclusionary. Everyone can choose to be chosen. This demonstrates that chosenness does not imply some innate superiority ascribed to Jews or some unwillingness to share the election by God. Jews may have been chosen as a special community to found a nation, follow God's Torah, and transmit a moral message, but it is a community open to all who wish to join it. In this sense, Judaism is a universal religion.

Beyond God's choice of the Jews, chosenness also includes the notion that the Jews freely chose to accept being chosen, to receive God's teaching. As the Talmud notes, "The Lord offered the Law to all nations; but all refused to accept it except Israel." Additionally, by tradition the Jewish people were willing to accept the responsibility of receiving God's moral teaching without demanding any particular privileges (Amos 3:2).

It still must be asked why God didn't simply provide a teaching meant for all humanity to all humanity. Just as a matter of efficiency, that seems to make more sense. Additionally, if the teaching is given to only one people, it seems likely, as eventually occurred, that other people would resent not being the ones to get the teaching and therefore would not listen to the Jews as they tried to offer God's moral message.

One possible response to this dilemma involves choice. If all people heard this message from God, there would be less spiritual choice about whether or not to follow the teaching. The fact that God's moral commands came from a small, powerless people increased the need to choose rather than just accept the teaching. Having just the Jewish people receive the message left room for doubt in two ways. Gentiles could doubt because they hadn't received the message directly. And Jews could doubt the message they had received because if it was so important why didn't others get it as well? Both Jews and Gentiles would therefore require faith to accept God's moral message.

It is easy to evade more troubling Jewish interpretations of chosenness such as that God believed the Jews had particular skills needed to receive the teaching or that by virtue of their patriarchal and matriarchal ancestors, the Jews had some kind of spiritual superiority. In the modern age built on such Enlightenment values as equality and tolerance the latter assertion is repulsive. Nevertheless such a view was central to the thought of the medieval Jewish thinker Judah Halevi and important for some other Jewish thinkers. This idea even comes wrapped in an attractive and charming package called the "Pintele Yid," which is Yiddish for "Jewish spark." It is, in Hasidic and other traditions, a holy spark that resides in every Jewish soul. This spark cannot be extinguished. Sometimes it does not burn brightly, but it is always present, always capable of burning again. This is a beautiful, even inspirational image, but note that in it is a view that the Jewish soul is somehow different from the Gentile soul. Precisely because of such views and that chosenness can be interpreted as God favoring the Jewish people, some modern Jewish thinkers have rejected the very idea of a chosen people. Mordecai Kaplan, the founder of Reconstructionism, is the most prominent of those thinkers. The other major movements in Judaism all accept some variation of chosenness.

Kaplan was a great believer in Jewish customs, and in the particularity of Jewish customs as a linchpin of preserving Jewish civilization. Jews may be called to perform their customs, but, according to Kaplan, they were not chosen to do so. Other Jewish thinkers joined Kaplan, seeing any assertion of chosenness as in contradiction with God's equal justice for all humans.

Modern Jews who wish to keep the useful notion of election need to do so by offering a precise explanation of it. It must be clear that a chosen people does not consider itself superior to others or exclusionary in refusing to let others join its people, that it does not seek to have others serve it but rather exists to serve others, that its chosenness is as much a matter of the Jewish people choosing God as God choosing the Jewish people, that chosenness is a powerful explanatory factor in understanding why it was that the Jews gave the world the idea of a single, good God, and that chosenness has come with a powerful burden for Jews in understanding it themselves and dealing with misunderstands by others.

As long as chosenness is understood with all these nuances and not applied in a way that excludes others or implies superiority or inequality, chosenness continues to have a central role in the Jewish belief system.

Chosenness is not an isolated concept. It is a link in a theological chain, and it leads logically to the next link: revelation.

After all, if God chose the Jews, that choice was for a reason and God had to reveal that reason to the Jewish people.

REVELATION

Revelation is so consequential because with the revealing of God's will we can apprehend what it is that God wants of us.

There were various forms and times of revelation in Jewish history. One form was to the founder of the Jewish people, Abraham, and the founder of Judaism, Moses, at the Burning Bush. Other personal revelations were made to the prophets. These prophets did not foretell the future but rather they served as messengers from God. They spoke to kings (King David, for example, listened to the prophet Nathan). Prophets also spoke to the nation. While we think of such prophets as Isaiah, Joel, Jeremiah, and others, it should be noted that women were also prophets. Rabbis in the Talmud thought Sarah, Miriam, Deborah, Hannah (who was Samuel the prophet's mother), Abigail (one of King David's wives), Huldah, and Esther were prophets. The great scholar Rashi added Rebecca, Rachel, and Leah, the matriarchs, along with Sarah, to the list of women prophets.

The communal revelation given to all who stood at the foot of Mount Sinai after the Exodus, the escape from slavery in Egypt, was the most significant revelation in Jewish history. Jewish traditionalists such as Orthodox Jews generally believe that there were two theophanies, divine manifestations, at Sinai. On this account God was manifest to all the people and then separately alone to Moses. Additionally, the revelation at Sinai came with Godly "language" through Moses. That is, God gave the Torah to the Israelites. (Traditionalists also believe that God gave Moses what became known as the Oral Torah, which was passed down until it found written form in the Mishnah and Talmud.)

The Torah, according to the traditional view, contains 613 mitzvot, or teachings or commandments that guide every aspect of Jewish behavior and in so doing engendered a sense of holiness.

This communal revelation raises various issues about God's choice of time and place. Why didn't God choose to give the Torah in the holy land of Israel? Or, even if the Torah is conceived, as it is by moderns, as wholly a human creation, why did the writers of the Torah not put the revelation in Israel?

In terms of its timing, the Torah's gift at a time of escape from slavery into freedom is a perfect metaphor of the Torah's place in human life. As God's revelation, it leads people from slavery to their natural instincts to freedom based on partnership with God. The Torah, on this interpretation, releases spiritual prisoners.

As to the location, the Torah was given in the desert, an area that belonged to no one. Therefore no one people, including Jews, could claim the Torah as only their own possession. God's message was given to Jews but meant for all humanity.

It is difficult to understand exactly what happened at the Sinai revelation. Of course, there are no problems for those who believe the Torah literally. What is written is what happened. But even the language is difficult to grasp. Consider, for example, the traditional notion that the Torah is from heaven, or, in Hebrew, *Torah Min Ha-Shamayim*. This phrase, suggesting the divine origins of the Torah, is nonetheless complicated. As the late British theologian Rabbi Louis Jacobs pointed out, we see the word *min* in a way familiar to Jews as part of the motzi, the blessing over bread. The end of that blessing is *"ha-motzi lechem min ha-aretz,"* or blessing God for "bringing forth bread from the Earth." As Rabbi Jacobs notes, no one thinks the bread emerged already toasted or already sliced. The bread from the Earth required human activity, and, Rabbi Jacobs concluded, so does the Torah from Heaven. Humans, that is, have a role in the shaping of the Torah.

The crucial question here can be summed up like this: Is Torah the literal word of God? If it is, the Torah should be followed as faithfully and fully as possible, for it contains the divine commands required of Jews to shape a moral and good life congruent with God's wishes and our own best interests.

The problem emerges if we don't think the Torah is literally from God. Almost all modern Jews reject a literal interpretation, seeing the Torah not as written down by Moses following God's direct instructions but as the work exclusively of humans, although humans who may have been inspired by God. But if the Torah is simply a collection of human words put together by an editor or redactor and declared sacred, then how can we regard the document as holy, and how can we say we have any revelation from God?

Is there a modernist approach to seeing the Torah as a meaningful revelation from God?

Such an approach might start with an appreciation of the limitations on language, including the sort of language God could use. That is, humans, being humans, with the biological limitations that implies and the limitations of human knowledge at the time of the giving of the Torah at Mount Sinai, could not comprehend all that God was capable of communicating. As a Midrash put it, "each Israelite heard what was in his power to hear." That is, whatever God was able to communicate could be either misheard or misunderstood, especially across time and space and cultures. Humans varied in their personal attributes and in the existing scientific, historical, and other knowledge and their grasp and comprehension of existing knowledge.

Additionally, suppose prophets had a profound comprehension of Godly revelation. Nevertheless, just as God presumably had to consider the skill level of his various listeners, so did the prophets who had to transmit the message. The prophets might have, that is, altered the revelation as they understood it to make it more comprehensible to those without prophetic abilities.

From this, a modernist could conclude that the Torah is a human response to God, an effort limited by humans with failings yet nevertheless eager and willing to hear the commanding voice of a living God. As a human record, the Torah is subject to constant reinterpretation on the assumption that emerging new knowledge and skills constantly clarifies the meaning of the divine message.

This notion coheres well with the Rabbinic interpretation of prophecy. After the end of the biblical era, the Rabbis declared the end of prophets, that the prophet was replaced by the sage, the learned reader and interpreter of text who could read the Torah or Talmud and explain its passages.

All this raises for modernists the troubling question of whether these human records and responses to divine revelation are sacred, that is whether or not they truly represent the divine will or simply the conjectures, prejudices, wisdom, and hopes of human beings.

Another interpretation of the Torah's revelation is to consider the Torah as revealed to separate prophets over time and edited together at one time to create a unifying document. For this interpretation to work, the prophets who received God's word must have been more than simply inspired. They must truly have received God's revelation—if by inspiration we mean ideas and thoughts that originated within the human mind by the human mind without getting the idea from God even if the prophet were thinking of God and truly believed the ideas came from God.

Beyond the direct revelation of the Torah as God's will, it is possible to consider revelation to individual human beings so that they understand the will of God in their own lives.

In any of these cases, for revelation to have truly occurred, it had to be directly communicated to human beings. Note that formally it is possible to believe in prophetic or personal revelation without believing that the Torah itself was divinely revealed or to believe that the Torah was divinely revealed and, like the Rabbis from the Talmudic Era, believe that no more revelation to humans currently occurs, that human reason and the interpretation of scripture provide appropriate access to God's will.

The event at Sinai, prophetic revelation, and personal revelation all imply what is sometimes called propositional revelation.

In a modern understanding of personal revelation, God's voice isn't external to a person's body but appears as one of the person's own thoughts that is recognized as God's thought and not the person's. In personal revelation, God "speaks" to people within their own minds. Revelation is silent speech. The people who receive God's thoughts must learn to discern between their own thoughts and God's.

If God communicates through ideas in the form of language to the human mind, and the communication is received in the human mind so that a thought dialogue with God can occur, there is a question beyond whether or not this is simply a psychological human event that is misinterpreted as a communication from God. That additional question is: How can God implant an idea from a distance to a particular mind and converse with the human or many humans simultaneously? Those who believe in propositional revelation might respond that God is, by definition, powerful enough to effect this revelation and that evolution of the brain gave humans the ability to have such mental religious encounters.

In Jewish literature, such a notion can be seen, for example, in the idea of a "soft, murmuring sound" (or, in another translation, "a still, small voice") (1 Kings 19:12).

This notion continues to be accepted by some modernist Jews and by some traditional Jews. For example, this statement is in the document *Emet Ve-Emunah: Statement of Principles of Conservative Judaism*: "Some of us conceive of revelation as the personal encounter between God and human beings. Among them there are those who believe that this personal encounter has propositional content, that God communicated with us in actual words. For them, revelation's content is immediately normative, as defined by rabbinic interpretation. The commandments of the Torah themselves issue directly from God."

Or consider the following from *The Thirteen Petalled Rose*, by the esteemed scholar Rabbi Adin Steinsaltz:

Sometimes man surrenders himself to the divine holiness only within the realm of Torah and *mitzvot*. And striving further, he may reach a certain identification with something that is known only in terms of the higher wisdom in him. If he should attain to a union of such great force, he is able to respond to the divine influence and be vouchsafed a revelation of the Holy Spirit, and his whole life would change accordingly. This level has indeed been achieved by many great men throughout history, through an adherence to *mitzvot* and Torah and by their whole way of life. And above this level are a select few who from time to time in human history are privileged to be so receptive to the divine plenty they are given prophetic power. And even with respect to prophetic power one may distinguish levels. There are prophets to whom prophecy comes as a transient vision: they feel as though a higher power compels them and produces in them images and ideas. On a higher level is the *Shekhinah* "who speaks in the throat," when all his life the prophet is in some connection with the divine will and he himself serves as an instrument of revelation. And at the highest level of holiness are those persons who have achieved a state in which their whole personalities and all of their actions are inseparably joined to the divine holiness. Of these persons it is said that they have become a "chariot" for the *Shekhinah*, and

like the Chariot, they are totally yielded up to the One who sits
on the driver's seat, the throne of glory, and they constitute a part
of the throne of glory itself, even though they are flesh and blood,
men like all other men.

It should be noted that some people consider what are perceived as personal revelations from God to in fact be a species
of self-deception or even madness, perhaps schizophrenia.
Schizophrenia, however, is frequently accompanied by symptoms that people who proclaim revelations don't always have,
such as hallucinations or delusions, disorganized and sometimes
incoherent speech, and a flattening of emotions.

Just because people have or believe they have propositional
revelations from God doesn't mean people will listen to them
or believe them. The biblical prophets were seen as speaking
for God, specially chosen to deliver a divine message or ethical teaching. Prophets were seen as holy people extraordinarily
close to God. *Navi* is the Hebrew word for "prophet." It means
"fruit of the lips," suggesting that the crucial role for the prophet
was speaking the message. That is, in a classical sense, propositional revelation was not meant for an individual but for all the
people with the individual delivering that message. According to
the Talmud, there were 1,200,000 prophets (twice the 600,000
people who left Egypt) in biblical times, but they were not all
recorded. The Bible lists fifty-five prophets, with Moses being
the greatest one.

Beyond propositional revelation, some people accept non-
propositional revelation such as the idea that God reveals divine
will through historical events or nature or in some way other
than a direct communication to humans.

Whatever modernists believe, the ancient Israelites believed
in revelation from Sinai and that overwhelming apprehension
led to an Israelite agreement with God, a contract to follow the

revelation in return for God's protection of the chosen people. This agreement is called a brit, or covenant.

COVENANT

The narrative of God's covenant with the Jewish people began with God's choosing Jews to serve as messengers of the holy teachings. The next step was the revelation of those teachings, either as traditionally understood through the Torah or through the prophets and later individual revelation or through not revelation but human inspiration. In the latter case, the Torah and other crucial Jewish texts were not revealed in any way and are therefore human creations, though perhaps separated from normal human creativity by the subject matter and the perception that the material emanated from an emotion, inspiration, that propelled an unsurpassed human creation. The Torah is the living embodiment between God and the Jewish people. That doesn't mean it is the literal word of God, but the way the Jewish people at the time understood and expressed both God's will and their own personal and communal missions.

Whether by revelation or inspiration, the Jewish people believed they had some kind of divine encounter and voluntarily had entered into a relationship with God.

In Exodus 19:3–6, God speaks to Moses telling him to offer a covenant to the Israelites. The Israelites, according to the terms of this agreement, will follow the laws of the Torah. That is, Halakhah, Jewish law, includes the full legal obligations incumbent upon Jews as given by God, at least as Jewish scholars understand and interpret them. In return the Israelites would be considered a treasured people. The Israelites accepted, and the revelation occurred three days later. God appeared before

all the people and spoke the Ten Commandments to them.
What is particularly interesting about the commandments is
that only the first four seem aimed particularly at the Israelites.
The final six are universal, indicating that the message was not
meant just for one small people. After the revelation to all the
people, Moses ascended into the darkness to receive more of
God's law before returning and telling the people. The covenant
was then ratified and Moses ordered that twelve pillars and an
altar be erected.

The covenant at Sinai was not the first biblical covenant. It
was an expansion, and a renewal, of the covenant God had made
with Abraham. But the very transformation of the covenant and
revelation from one person to an entire people was unique in
human history. From an American perspective, one steeped in
individualism and self-reliance, it is easy to miss the full implications of the revelation being given to the whole people. Such
a revelation moves the moral and legal responsibility from individuals to the people to obey the rules God revealed. Additionally, it is crucial not to reduce the revelation to a series of rules
about, for example, keeping the Sabbath or following dietary
restrictions. The revelation was not simply about the practices
required for worship. The revelation included a substantial
number of moral regulations making good behavior obligatory.
These moral rules extended far beyond the usual borders of religious regulation. They included rules for individuals as members of a social order. The revelation by God illustrates God's
concerns are moral not just ceremonial, that behaving morally
is at least as important to God as keeping rituals.

The covenant makes the Jewish people and individual Jews
partners with God. This partnership exists not so the Jews can
simply worship God but so they can create the sort of world
both God and the people desire, one characterized by peace,
justice, opportunity, love, and kindness.

How Jews act as God's partner depends in large part on how they interpret the whole idea of revelation and their responsibility to act on it. For traditionalists, including Orthodox and Conservative Jews, the rules of the revelation, the 613 mitzvot, are binding, and the defining role of the covenant is to interpret Halakhah correctly so that we can obey the mitzvot. This means that the Torah has the ultimate authority in Jewish life, and we must revolve around its proclamations, for it defines the will of God.

For the traditional Jew, Halakhah provides a comprehensive guide to a good life in covenant with God. Halakhic emphasis is not on right belief but on right behavior, and so the Halakhah is a guidebook with rules and practices. What can Jews eat and what foods are forbidden? What behaviors are forbidden on the Sabbath, the day of rest? How are all the holy days observed? What are the rules for marriage, for running a business?

To the modern ear, the Halakhah can be misinterpreted as simply a rigid set of rules that must be followed. Such an outlook misses the immense spiritual dimensions of the Halakhah. The way of life the Halakhah represents transforms the ordinary into the sacred. It lifts life from the dull to the meaningful. Observing the rules of Halakhah provides for those who do so an ongoing relationship to God, a constant sense of the meaning of life.

Some modern Conservative Jews believe that the Torah was created by humans as a response to what they understood the revelation from God to be. But if the Torah is from humans and not God, then the Torah does not have the ultimate authority in Jewish life. If the Jewish people created the Torah, then those qualified to study its rules—the Rabbis—are the focus of authority.

Reform Jews believe that the Torah was created by inspired humans, that its rules are subject to be changed, and that individuals are guided by their own education and conscience forms the locus of authority in Jewish life.

These, of course, are broad generalizations and there is a very wide variation within groups and among individuals.

Franz Rosenzweig, for example, understood God as having a presence in a personal relationship with humans. This presence took the form of commanding actions. If we consider the notion of covenant, we might understand Rosenzweig as implying that God and individual Jews join together to define appropriate moral activities and then the individuals act based on that joint effort.

For modern thinkers, there can be an understanding that the more humans learn, the more any past or current revelations are understood. We as individuals judge if traditional revelations or assertions by contemporary Jews that some message has been revealed to them cohere with contemporary knowledge, our personal experiences, and the basic beliefs of Judaism.

It should also be noted that the Jewish attachment to the Land of Israel is part of the covenant (Genesis 17:18).

The human efforts to act on God's revelation, to meet the covenantal agreement, can be called a mission.

JEWISH MISSIONS

Mission is a confusing word in many ways. The word comes from the Reform movement. In a sense it was a way of transforming the older notion of the chosen people to mean chosen to serve. It is meant to imply duty, assignment, goal, task, errand, purpose, pursuit, or vocation. Any of these synonyms could just as well be used. Part of the confusion involving the word *mission* comes from its use in Christianity where it centers on efforts to seek converts. In a Jewish sense, though, a mission is a holy task and moral responsibility.

For traditionalists, the mission is identical to keeping the mitzvot. For modern Jews, the task of defining a communal mission as well as any supplementary individual missions is more complex.

Part of the difficulty arises in attempting to define a communal mission apart from Halakhah. At the same time, however, Halakhah is not accepted by all Jews either. Therefore, because there is no central authority in Judaism and because there is no universally accepted communal mission, the honest effort to participate in the covenant is a difficult one. There are many people, for example, who do not believe in God, or in revelation, or feel disconnected from prayers and rituals even while continuing to attend services.

One alternative answer is to consider Judaism as a special kind of belief system, one that includes moral activities. For the Orthodox those activities overlap Halakhic mandates. But for modernist Jews, seeing Judaism as a belief system can provide a cohesion not available through the traditional method of observing 613 commandments as understood to be contained in the Torah.

Seeing Judaism as a belief system reduces the dissonance between Halakhah, a regulated behavioral system, and regulation by an individual conscience. The regulated system is one of belief and the conscience determines how to structure activities that support that belief.

A belief system by definition does not have its own rituals beyond reading, thinking, perhaps writing down the belief system, and discussing it with others. That is, no belief system negates any traditional Jewish rituals, so that individuals and groups with belief systems will look for which rituals are meaningful within the system and provide a representation of its values.

With this interpretation, individual Jews have multiple missions, communal and personal ones. One limitation on individual

missions, though, is that they can't be contradictory to Jewish communal missions.

The purpose of life can be understood as people searching for, finding, and fulfilling their missions. These continually emerge throughout a person's life so that efforts involving missions are lifelong efforts. New missions can occur at different ages. Often a mature mission is understood most clearly only after an adequate number of years have been lived.

Besides Halakhah, what can count as communal and personal modern missions for the Jewish people? The foundational problem is to define the authority for the construction of a list of modern missions. One answer, of course, is each person's conscience, but this is chaotic when it comes to forming communal missions and seeing the connection between such communal missions and individual ones. Clearly, in structuring such a list the contemporary needs and wants of the Jewish people must be considered. Some missions, such as the support of the nation of Israel, have widespread appeal, but some missions might be important for Jewish survival but not so well known. The only clear approach is a democratic one. Ideas for a list of modern missions need to be put forth for consideration by Jews, and they can freely choose whether or not to adopt the missions. Those ideas need to include justifications for each mission, and for the idea of mission itself. For example, the very existence of missions is an argument against passivity, which has proven again and again in Jewish history to be dangerous.

In that spirit, following is one possible list of modern Jewish missions.

I. A Demographic Mission

The first commandment in the Torah is to "be fruitful and multiply." Put in more contemporary terms, especially after the

loss of one-third of the Jewish people during the Holocaust, is that Jewish life cannot continue without enough Jews. There is much dispute about the number of Jews in the United States. The number varies greatly depending on who is counted as being Jewish and the methodology of the counting. But some facts can't be denied: the aging American Jewish population, the increasing percentage of the Orthodox, especially in New York City, the declining percentage of Jews compared to the overall American population, and so on. In Israel, there is an ongoing demographic competition between Israeli Arabs and Israeli Jews. Demography is destiny in a democracy. Israel's future, its politics, economics, religion, and culture, will be determined by who votes in elections and through that controls the nation's principal institutions.

Therefore, the first communal and personal missions have to be demographic.

There are only a limited number of ways to increase the Jewish population. In Israel the main efforts have been through increasing Jewish births and immigration. But pronatalism, or, birth encouragement, has limits. David Ben-Gurion proposed that the Israeli government provide a cash bonus to every Israeli woman who gave birth to a tenth child. The plan was discontinued after a large number of Arab women collected the bonus. The Israeli government, as a democracy, was obligated to give equal treatment to every citizen.

Birth encouragement will not work in the United States either, at least among the non-Orthodox, who currently make up the overwhelming majority of American Jews. The efforts that are most likely to succeed involve attracting new Jews, such as those with Jewish ancestors and, especially, welcoming converts to Judaism. This effort will be considered as a separate mission below.

On a personal level this mission means, when it is possible, to have children, support efforts to enhance adoptions by Jewish families, and so on.

2. A Religious Mission

While Judaism is more than a religion, its religious component is vital. Such a component involves celebrating and remembering being Jewish, for example, by observing holidays such as having a seder during Passover or keeping the Sabbath. This mission is especially important because Judaism can't survive just as a series of beliefs. That's precisely what makes Judaism a special kind of belief system rather than an ordinary one. People need reminders about being Jewish.

The religious mission includes engaging in personal and communal prayer, joining and supporting synagogues and other religious institutions including media, studying religious texts, following chosen religious rituals, and so on. It would be valuable for members of different religious groups to read the prayer books of the other groups, attend their services, read books about them, and in other ways expand an understanding so that the Jewish people remains united but not identical.

The religious mission can, of course, be carried out in the traditional way by observing the 613 commandments of the Torah. Another way of looking at the religious mission is to define which particular observances to follow and define new observances to reflect contemporary beliefs. There are some ceremonies, for example, for the new moon, Rosh Chodesh. In particular, some women gather in Rosh Chodesh groups and explore issues and activities of interest and concern to Jewish women.

3. An Educational Mission

To fulfill their mission, Jews have to know Judaism. They have to read the holy texts and know the history and culture of modern Judaism. Not everyone needs to or can become a scholar, but a pedagogical task requires mastery of the material taught. If Jews have a covenantal mission to teach Judaism, they ought to make studying it a basic part of their overall mission.

On a personal level, this mission requires a commitment to regular study, providing a sound and extensive Jewish education for one's children, and supporting Jewish institutions that teach, such as synagogues, Jewish Community Centers, day schools, camps, and so on.

4. A Jewish Communal Mission

This mission involves supporting the institutions that make up the Jewish community, such as organizations and media. Support involves philanthropy, as well as joining and getting involved with Jewish organizations.

5. A Cultural Mission

The cultural mission mandates supporting products of Jewish culture, such as books, movies, art, music, and humor. It also includes creating culture when possible. Cultural products help people connect to the Jewish heritage and people and define themselves. Culture offers simultaneously a sense of belonging by a recognition of the cultural product's meaning but also an opportunity to question and challenge by the rebelliousness in some cultural products. Works of art create symbols that provide alternate ways of understanding, alternate paths to the center of meaning. Such works can make us laugh or cry. They can provide shocks of recognition when we realize we are connected to Jewish life in ways we hadn't previously realized until the work of art made us aware.

6. A Humanitarian Mission

Followers of all streams of Judaism, and secular Jews, believe in the Jewish requirement to be humane, to, for example, help the poor, sick, and homeless, the widows and orphans. Judaism also stresses concern for animals.

Many in the Reform movement have focused on the term *tikkun olam* ("repair of the world") as a principal mission of Jewish life. The concept arose in the Talmudic period and was transformed by Kabbalistic thinkers. The phrase appears in the Aleinu prayer.

7. A National Mission

There is only one Jewish nation, one place where Jews can go for refuge and be welcomed just because they are Jewish, one place where the Hebrew language and Jewish culture flourishes, one nation that stands on the ancient sacred land of the ancestors of the contemporary Jewish people. It is therefore no surprise that supporting Israel is a crucial contemporary Jewish mission.

It is worthwhile to recapitulate the ways in which the existence of Israel has transformed the Jewish people and the Gentile perceptions of Jews.

Throughout much of their history since 70 CE when the Second Temple was destroyed, the Jews were considered apostates who would not accept the Christian God, or in other ways religious outsiders. The Jews were considered inferior, below Gentiles in social standing and in God's eyes. The course of Jewish history, so often punctuated by dispossession, dispersion, the absence of any military or political strength, and brutal attacks, seemed to many Gentiles to confirm the religious prejudice they held. Beginning in the nineteenth century, religious prejudice was supplemented by and in some sense replaced by a belief in Jewish racial inferiority. This transformation was crucial. A person could change a religion, but people could not change their "race." Israel's rebirth is a form therefore of historical vindication. God and history have not abandoned the Jews. The Gentile perception was incorrect.

Israel's rebirth has revived the Jewish spirit. That spirit, so tested by history, was warped but miraculously intact. It was savaged, but it was still alive. It was stymied in its attempts to redeem the world, but still chosen to do so. When history vindicates deeply held beliefs such as the return to Zion, a people gets energized. When reality stunningly verifies deeply buried hopes, then emotional wellsprings erupt leading to increased pride, a confirmation of divine purpose, and renewed confidence. As David Ben-Gurion, Israel's founding prime minister, put it, "in Israel, in order to be a realist one must believe in miracles."

The birth of Israel also eroded various triumphalist notions of non-Jewish religions. It was not true that all of Judaism's glories were in the past. It was not true that Judaism's religious assertions had been superseded by other religions. It was not true that the Jews were just vestigial, history's fossils.

Israel provides a spiritual, national, cultural, and political center to Jewish life. In Israel the Jewish heritage vibrates with growth. Israel is the model of the spiritual quest shaped into the concrete forms of the actual. If Israel had as a mission to be a light to the nations, it is also true that a light needs a safe place to stand.

Israel provides a place where Jews in trouble can come home. No Jew after the Holocaust can demean the importance of such a fact.

Zionists perceived Diaspora history as a deep valley in Jewish life. In a sense it was, because once a Jewish nation was reestablished Jews were psychologically more prepared and historically more vindicated to revive their covenantal obligations.

The Orthodox had not seen Israel as necessary. The obligation was met by observing the mitzvot and through doing that providing a model. The Reform movement began mostly in opposition to Zionism because Reform Jews saw spreading

Jewish ideas as the divine obligation and living in the Diaspora provided Jews the opportunity to reside in many lands to teach about Judaism. The Reform movement gradually transformed its views and now, like the modern Orthodox, most traditional Orthodox, and the Conservative movement, sees Israel as vital to the Jewish people's survival.

Communal and personal missions regarding Israel include deciding how best to help Israel. For some people, up to now a very small percentage of the American Jewish population, that means making aliyah, or moving to Israel. For others it means supporting Israel by traveling there, say for a child's bat or bar mitzvah, or giving financial support, or getting involved in pro-Israel political activities such as by supporting a pro-Israel organization such as the American Israel Public Affairs Committee (AIPAC) or a pro-Israel political action committee, or working for or volunteering for a pro-Israel candidate, or even running for political office.

8. A Mission to Welcome Converts to Judaism

This mission is not as well known as the others, but it deserves a full explanation. According to this interpretation of mission, the Jewish people, having received God's message to all humanity, have a moral obligation to offer that message and welcome sincere converts who voluntarily accept the moral message. It is important to stress that the idea of welcoming does not include any implicit or explicit threats, deceit, unwanted attempts at persuasion, bribes, or coercion. It does not, for example, include violating someone's privacy such as by knocking on their front door and offering Judaism or demeaning other faiths in any way. Welcoming means to make knowledge of Judaism available such as through literature, films, classes, lectures, and so on, and responding in a kindly manner to those who inquire about becoming Jewish.

The prophetic vision of undertaking a mission (Isaiah 2:2–4; Micah 4:1–4; Tobit 13:11) was for humans to accept the moral instruction that came from Zion and then turn to God. It was this turning that would result in an era of world peace.

Rabbi Hillel is the model Talmudic figure when it comes to welcoming converts. In one statement, he said, "Be of the disciples of Aaron . . . loving people and drawing them near to the Torah." Also in the Talmud there are famous stories about Hillel and converts. The most famous one involves a Gentile who approached another Rabbi named Shammai. The Gentile wanted to convert to Judaism but insisted on being taught the whole Torah while he stood on one foot. Shammai saw that the man was mocking and so rejected him. The Gentile then went to Hillel and made the same request. Hillel granted the request, and said to the man: "That which is hateful to you, do not do to others. That is the basis of the Torah. The rest is commentary. Go forth and study." This welcoming attitude, even of a mocking pagan, is a significant model for contemporary Jews. Note also that Hillel's rule is similar to but not exactly the so-called Golden Rule: "Do unto others as you would have others do unto you." Hillel's negative formulation is more precise. Consider, for example, a masochist. Since the masochist enjoys pain, following the Golden Rule mandates inflicting pain on others. But that is not the case following Hillel's rule.

Rabbi Johanan had another important statement, one in which he praised conversionary work by using it to justify the exile from the Land of Israel, saying the Jews were exiled from their homeland for only one reason, to increase the number of converts.

The Jewish people, when legally allowed and when they didn't face persecution for doing so, actively and eagerly welcomed converts. They created missionary literature, invited Gentiles to enter and learn in synagogues, engaged in religious discussions with those who had questions, assimilated Gentiles who settled among them, and converted those who married into the Jewish people.

It is important to add that in offering Judaism, the Jewish people did not belittle Gentiles or claim that it was necessary to become Jewish in order to achieve salvation, or to be considered righteous. The most famous passage illustrating this is from the Tosefta of Sanhedrin, chapter 13: "The righteous of all nations shall have a portion in the world to come."

In modern Jewish life, it was the Reform movement that focused on welcoming converts, although there are severe disagreements among the movements about conversionary issues such as who can perform a conversion and the requirements for legal conversion. Part of this mission, then, is to seek ways to overcome these differences.

9. A Redemptive Mission

The ultimate goal of the Jewish missions is to create an ideal world. This concept is summed up in the word *redemption*. In Jewish history this in practical terms has meant confronting idolatry, or serving as a living example, or actively seeking converts to Judaism. More abstractly, redemption refers to the reconciliation of humanity with God so that God is not disappointed in the moral behavior of people but rather relieved that human moral potential has been fulfilled. Such a transformation would justify God's original plan to create humans as partners to make a moral world. The human enterprise would have found its ultimate meaning. In a state of redemption, humans will be released from sin and therefore emotional suffering.

All the above and other potential missions require fulfillment. That means developing individual and communal priorities about time, funding, and personnel used for specific missions.

For individuals, that development of priorities is supplemented by learning and acquiring skills to start and work at the mission, joining with others such as in an organization to work together on missions, defining the steps needed for the mission, and doing the actual work. Some missions will be completed; many are likely not to be completed, but in the words of Rabbi Tarfon in the Talmud, "The day is short, the labor vast, the toilers idle, the reward great, and the Master urgent. You are not obliged to complete the work, but neither are you free to evade it."

Missions can be understood as voluntary undertakings, but they can alternately be understood as ethically obligatory. As such, they might be seen as the contemporary example of the mitzvot. The missions are the practices.

There are psychological dimensions to the missions. They are, after all, performed by people. In the Bible many prophets were convinced they were incapable of performing their mission, as was Moses, or they ran away from their mission, as did Jonah. Missions can be daunting, frightening, anxiety producing, guilt inducing, and overwhelming. In a way, in Jewish history there is a tug between responsibility to perform the missions on the one hand and anxiety on the other. This very human struggle, seen in Israel's greatest prophets and in ordinary people, has no clear resolution other than people have the obligation to do what they are capable of doing. Not more, but not less either.

ETHNIC DIVISIONS

It's not easy to define who is or isn't Jewish. Is someone with a Jewish father and Gentile mother who keeps all 613 commandments Jewish? Not according to Halakhah. Is a person who has a Jewish mother and Gentile father Jewish? Yes, according to

Halakhah. And Jewish legal issues involving status and conversion, for example, are just part of the problem.

Modernity has complicated the issue even more. Consider the story of the visitor who has returned from Israel and talks to a friend. The first man reports that in Israel he met a Jew who studied at a very Orthodox yeshiva and had memorized much of the Talmud. Then he met a Jew who was an agnostic. He said he met a Jew who had a large toy business and a Jew who was an avid socialist. His friend noted that Israel had many Jews with much variety. "You don't understand," the visitor said. "These were all the same Jew." We have divided selves, and the psychological pressures on all people are compounded for minorities in America, including Jews.

Additionally, the Jewish people have many ethnic groups. To oversimplify, the Ashkenazim, for example, have ancestors who spoke Yiddish and came from Germany at one time. The Ashkenazim make up about three-quarters of the Jewish people. The Sephardim have ancestors who spoke Ladino and lived in Spain or Portugal. The Mizrahim have ancestors who were from the Middle East or North Africa. And there are several other, smaller groups in addition to these.

That is, the Jewish people are a diverse lot, not united by any single reality. That's why it's crucial to understand them as bound either by traditional Halakhah or by a belief system.

EXERCISES

Make your own list of modern missions. Make a list of steps to take for you to fulfill those missions.

Consider whether or not you believe in personal revelation, such as the ancient prophets received. The section on propositional revelation was very difficult for me to write because of an incident in my life. I'm cautious as I write about such possible personal, propositional revelation. When I was young, I lived in an apartment with three other young men. One of them murdered his father. I never did get a chance to speak to him, but his lawyer told me that he had heard the voices of God and Jimi Hendrix (who was not then dead) telling him to stab his father. Ever since then I've been careful as I discuss people who claim to hear from God and emphasize that any purported messages need to cohere with human morality and, as I wrote, Jewish morality.

Do you believe in angels? Although angels aren't mentioned in the Mishnah, there are a lot of references to them elsewhere in Rabbinic literature and, of course, in the Bible. In the literature angels have several characteristics. They exist eternally. They cannot reproduce. They, unlike humans, have no evil urges. It should also be noted that they are not to be worshipped. Worship is for God alone. Generally, angels do not have names, although there are the exceptions of Gabriel and Michael. Modern Jews have either abandoned or downplayed the belief in angels (or in demons for that matter, other beings popular in the Rabbinic materials). The powers of these beings have alternative modern explanations. No longer do most people believe a demon's invasion of the human mind is the cause of mental aberrations.

As with much else, individual Jews, based on their experiences, can believe or not believe in such beings. Questions such as what purpose they serve or whether or not God needs them do not trouble modern theologians but individual believers may find a place in their worldview, especially for angels as messengers of God.

Here is a small list of some people who have converted to Judaism. Their experiences can help you think about Judaism.

Abraham and Sarah—the first Jewish couple. That is, everyone who is Jewish is descended from a couple in which
neither partner was born Jewish.

Ruth—the great-grandmother of King David, and therefore,
by tradition, an ancestor of the Messiah

Onkelos—an ancient scholar

Warder Cresson—the first U.S. consul to Jerusalem, and the
most important convert in America during the nineteenth
century. When he returned to America to tell his family
he had decided to become Jewish, they had him declared
insane. His trial became national news. He was declared
sane and moved to the Land of Israel where he did become Jewish.

Reuel Abraham—a former Luftwaffe pilot. He was born Karl
Heinz Schneider and was member of the Hitler Youth.
It was while he was in Poland that Schneider saw SS
members murder a group of Jews. After that, Schneider
feigned illness to escape participating in combat missions,
deliberately missed targets he had been ordered to hit,
and tampered with his airplane's bombs so that they would
not detonate. After the war, he worked as a coal miner for
two decades, anonymously donating much of his income to
Jewish survivors and orphans. He immigrated to Israel in
1965 and changed his name to Reuel Abraham. Eventually
he converted to Judaism.

Marilyn Monroe—entertainer and one-time wife of play-
wright Arthur Miller

Elizabeth Taylor—entertainer

Sammy Davis Jr.—entertainer

Ivanka Trump—business leader

Kate Capshaw—entertainer and wife of director Steven
Spielberg

Daniel Silva—author

Imagine that you are planning to convert to Judaism and are appearing in front of a Bet Din, a religious court. One of the rabbis asks you why you want to become Jewish. What is your answer?

Read about Israel. The nation is important to Jews for many reasons. These include the traditional notion that it is the Promised Land. But it was also the ancestral land and, in a more modern sense, the only nation on Earth that did and can provide refuge for any Jew who needs physical safety.

There are many stories about the creation of the Jewish State. Here is one about Golda Meir (1898–1978), who eventually became the prime minister of Israel.

In the aftermath of the November 1947 United Nations vote for partition and the creation of two states in the Land of Israel, there was a great need for weapons. Some of these weapons were available on the black market or from Communist countries such as Czechoslovakia that were anxious to oust Britain from the Middle East.

The weapons cost a lot of money, a sum so vast that it was beyond the Zionist movement's capacity to raise it. David Ben-Gurion, then in charge, determined that such funds were only available in the United States. Although he was desperately needed at home to plan for the new Jewish nation, he saw no alternative but to go to America. Golda Meir, a member of the cabinet, thought Ben-Gurion was needed just where he was, and so, reluctantly, she volunteered to undertake the mission. Ben-Gurion, however, refused her offer. Golda was, to put it mildly, determined. "No one can take your place here, while I may be able to do what you can do in the United States." But Ben-Gurion would not budge. Golda wouldn't back down. She called for a vote on the matter. Ben-Gurion stared hard at her and finally agreed to the vote. Golda won the vote and left that same day, without luggage, wearing the dress she had worn to the cabinet meeting. Her goal, seemingly impossible to reach, was to raise $5 million. Even that was low in terms of need for the weapons, but no one thought such a number could be reached.

Golda first appeared in Chicago on January 21, 1948, at the general assembly of the Council of Jewish Federations and Welfare Funds, which was not a Zionist group. The audience consisted of professional fund-raisers. Golda was exhausted. She had not rehearsed her speech. She feared that the audience was not familiar with Zionism, that it was not very high on their agenda. She was there without being either scheduled or announced. No one was prepared to hear a woman pleading for money for a faraway land when there were so many needs in the United States.

Golda approached the microphone with a single thought. She had to ask for all the money that was needed, not just the $5 million, even if she had been told that even that number couldn't be reached. She began by telling the crowd that the Jews in what would be the new Jewish State would fight to the end. They would use stones if they had to do so. She said that the Zionist leaders needed somewhere between $25 and $30 million within the next few weeks. She said that the Jewish people in the Land of Israel had made their decision. Now the people in the audience had a decision to make as well. Their dollars would determine whether the Jews or the Arabs won the fight.

People in the audience began weeping. Then they began giving.

Golda remained in the United States for six weeks. She traveled and spoke all over the country. People gave. They took out loans so they could give more.

In March 1948 Golda Meir returned to her people. She had raised $50 million. An agent in Paris notified Ben-Gurion that he could buy tanks but they would cost $10 million, Golda's money was used. In Czechoslovakia, there were planes and heavy guns that could be purchased. Golda's money was used. When Golda returned home, it was Ben-Gurion, as usual, who summed it up best: "Some day, when history will be written, it will be said that there was a Jewish woman who got the money which made the state possible."

Support Israel in any way you wish. This can include visiting Israel, buying Israeli products, contributing to Israeli organizations or to American organizations that support Israel such as AIPAC, the American Israel Public Affairs Committee, contributing to a pro-Israel political action committee, and so on.

Every congregational member can join the pro-Israel organization set up by its movement.

At my congregation, we focused on a prayer for Gilad Shalit during his captivity. Shalit, who was born in 1986, was a soldier in the IDF (Israel Defense Forces) and was kidnapped inside Israel on June 25, 2006, by terrorists from Hamas who had crossed the border into Israel on a raid by going through the underground tunnels. Gilad was held for more than five years. Eventually he was released on October 18, 2011, in a deal involving prisoner exchanges.

During the time he was held, each Sabbath in our synagogue, the Rabbi led a prayer for Gilad. In that way, we consistently reminded ourselves that he was still a prisoner, and each week we steeled our resolve to support him. The prayer led to talk about him and about Israel.

There are an enormous number of activities that individuals and communities can do for Israel, and all are important.

⑦

THE JEWISH SELF

Ethical Foundations for a Good Life

ETHICAL MODELS

There is a popular Jewish legend that thirty-six just people (in tradition, the reference is to men, but a modern understanding includes all people) save the rest of humanity from destruction. These thirty-six ethical, honest, righteous people justify the continued existence of human beings in God's eye. The origins of the legend go back to an effort to explain what occurred after the Flood in the Bible. In that account, God promised Noah that there would be no more attempts to destroy the Earth. God supposedly created the rainbow as a recurrent sign of the promise. Still, God was aware that humans could and would continue to be wicked. Therefore, God sought an additional way to ensure that the Earth would not be destroyed.

According to the legend, God then created seventy-two just people. Thirty-six of them stayed in Heaven. Their job was to plead for mercy on behalf of a troubled humanity. The other thirty-six were to come down and live on Earth. It is because of their good work that God spares all humans.

By tradition, these thirty-six just people remain hidden. They perform their good deeds without anyone learning of their significance. They may be poor. They may be without an education. But they are kind. The ethical lesson is that we should treat all people well because any one of them may be one of the thirty-six.

Jews point with pride to those with ethical bravery.

Abraham Zelmanowitz died heroically in the World Trade Center on September 11, 2001. President George W. Bush said of him, "We have seen our national character in eloquent acts of sacrifice. Inside the World Trade Center, one man who could have saved himself stayed until the end and at the side of his quadriplegic friend."

Zelmanowitz worked as a computer programmer for Empire Blue Cross Blue Shield, located in Tower One of the World Trade Center, on the twenty-seventh floor. When the plane hit his building, he could have left, but doing so would have meant leaving his friend, Edward Beyea, a quadriplegic. The elevators had ceased to work, and Beyea could not leave the building. The staff left, but Zelmanowitz chose to remain behind with his friend, hoping that rescue workers would arrive in time. Those workers, however, could not reach the people still trapped.

The two friends died together that day. Many of their friends thought they prayed during those final moments. Zelmanowitz was an Orthodox Jew and Beyea was a devout Roman Catholic.

Abraham Zelmanowitz's remains were buried about a year later in Jerusalem at the Mount of Olives cemetery.

Here is another Jewish story of moral behavior. The story was told by the late Rabbi Gerald I. Wolpe and is paraphrased here. Wolpe recalled a moment in his youth when he needed someone's help. The young boy was eleven when his father died. Each morning he stopped halfway to school at a synagogue where he could recite the kaddish. The other congregants overlooked the fact that, since young Wolpe wasn't yet thirteen, he could not be counted as part of the minyan, the quorum necessary to recite the prayer. After a week of Wolpe attending the minyan, the synagogue's shamash, someone who assists in the running of the congregation, appeared at Wolpe's door. The shamash, Mr. Einstein, said that he was walking to the synagogue and the boy's home was on the way. Einstein said he thought it would be fun to have some company so that he wouldn't have to walk alone. He asked Wolpe if he might be allowed to walk along with him. Together the pair trudged through the New England snows, the rain, the humidity of summer, and each morning Mr. Einstein would teach as they walked, telling the boy stories of Jewish life. The pair sat next to each other during the services.

Many years passed, and the two stayed in touch. Gerald Wolpe became a rabbi. Mr. Einstein was by then in his nineties. Rabbi Wolpe called one day and said he wished to show his new son to Mr. Einstein. The old shamash said he could not go anywhere but invited the rabbi and his family to the Einstein home. Rabbi Wolpe realized he had never known where that home was, and so got the address.

As he drove, Rabbi Wolpe got more and more shocked. The shamash's home was not near the Wolpe home at all. Mr. Einstein had to walk for an hour to get to the boy's home so young Wolpe would not have to walk alone. The shamash had said the walking together was a favor to him when all along it was a great favor to the boy so the forlorn youngster would not have to walk alone.

Rabbi Wolpe realized that Mr. Einstein had taken a sad young boy and led him back into life.

Beyond being members of a people, each Jewish person is an individual and as an individual has a particular life, with its challenges and personal goals and missions. Individual Jews have moments of struggle and ecstasy. Their character emerges in moments of confusion and distress, as it did for Abraham Zelmanowitz or Mr. Einstein. For those and more ordinary moments, Jews can, if they choose, be guided by the ethical insights accumulated by Judaism across the millennia. As Rabbi Louis Finkelstein once put it, "a good Jew is someone who is always trying to be a better Jew."

Jewish ethics emanate from Jewish beliefs and from the Jewish way of life, which includes rites, ceremonies, observances, and customs. Beliefs about God; about what kind of beings humans are, especially in regard to free will; and about the role of the Jewish people in history affect the ethical lessons that Judaism has to offer to the world.

The language of morality is sometimes unclear. Some people draw a distinction between morality and ethics. Morality refers to questions of what is right or wrong, or what is good or bad. Here are two examples of moral questions: Is it right for someone to steal a loaf of bread if the person's child is hungry? Is it right for a nation to attack first if it knows it is going to be attacked by another nation? Ethics involves questions about the nature of morality. What is the difference between right and wrong? How does our morality develop? Morality is practical and specific; ethics is abstract. This book deals almost exclusively with morality, practical issues of human behavior even when the word *ethics* is used for stylistic reasons.

It is also useful to see ethical subdivisions within Jewish ethics. Values is one of those divisions. A moral value states an ethical principle or an ideal. Peace is a value. Justice is a value. A moral virtue is a specific quality of a person marking the person as moral. Kindness is a virtue. Patience is a virtue. Moral rules are the obligations we have to follow in order to lead a moral life. One famous Jewish moral rule is to honor your parents. Note that moral rules are more precisely defined than the more abstract values and virtues. Also, it is often the case that particular moral examples fit into more than one of these categories. As with the distinction between *ethics* and *morality*, the borderlines among the different subdivisions are not always noted in this book because they meet and mix so readily in real life.

There are various moral actions for a human to take within the Jewish tradition. These will be enumerated below. But it should be clear that while specific actions are crucial, the goal of getting people to behave morally includes a deeper goal to get people to develop a moral character, the ability to react reflexively with upright behavior. Jews are considered free moral agents and, as such, they bear responsibility for their actions. They can justifiably be judged for their behavior.

The concept of a Jewish ethics implies that humans, however morally gifted they may be, are incapable of fully seeing the entire moral landscape and so need guidance as they make their journey through life. That is, humans need to be in partnership with God and follow God's teachings rather than relying simply on human intuition in order to make moral decisions. This is what separates Judaism from, say, humanism, which asserts that humans not only are alone in the cosmos but also have sufficient moral knowledge and are capable of adequate judgment to guide their own lives without acknowledging or attempting to access Godly ethical direction.

The term *Jewish morality* is misleading. The morality applied to Jews is applied to all. While Jews have special commandments, the mitzvot, the principles of moral behavior apply to all people.

Judaism is sometimes understood as ethical monotheism because moral actions are considered so crucial, so much at the center of a Jewish self-understanding of its own faith.

Perhaps the most important of the many ethical guides in traditional Judaism is from the Mishnah. It is Pirkei Avot, often translated as "Ethics of the Fathers." There are many famous moral injunctions in the work such as, "If I am not for myself, who will be for me? And when I am for myself, what am I? And if not now, when?" (1:14). Because ethics is such an important subject in biblical literature, there are other works in Jewish history on right and wrong. And yet, paradoxically, the focus of Jewish writing centered more on Jewish law. The first book exclusively devoted to Jewish ethics did not appear until the eleventh century. This was *Duties of the Heart* by Bahya Ibn Pakuda. There was a body of ethical literature produced in the thirteenth century. One important ethical movement arose in Lithuania in the Orthodox movement. Israel Salanter founded the Musar movement. Followers of this movement believed that moral precepts had been neglected with all religious attention paid to ritual demands.

Below are some of the principal precepts that make up Jewish morality. Together they constitute the true north of our moral compass. This chapter includes a focus on personal moral virtues and obligations. Social virtues and obligations, including contemporary issues, will be covered in chapter 9, which is about community.

Some of these virtues have a religious meaning.

Imitation of God

The goal of imitating God, insofar as it can be comprehended and applied, is to behave as God would in a particular moral situation. Since God is morally perfect, this goal is literally unattainable, but its presence is intended to promote the highest standards of good actions. The origins of the idea stem from the notion that humans are created in God's image. Since God has no physicality, this can't mean a physical resemblance but must instead mean a moral resemblance. There is a bodily dimension, though, to the imitation of God. If humans are made in God's image, Jews are obligated to honor their own physical selves by taking care of the body they have, for in some respect, it is in the image of God even if only in the sense of being the container of the soul or mind or consciousness that connects the human and the divine.

Holiness (*Kedushah*)

Holiness implies a separation from the profane. Therefore God is holy. Places, such as Jerusalem, can be seen as holy. In terms of the Jewish people, *holy* means that the people need to be distinguishable from others such as by the rituals they keep, the commandments they obey, and by their exemplary moral behavior.

This separation, however, does not imply that Jews should separate themselves from a profane world. The Jewish ideal is to engage with the world, to work as God's partner to improve the world, not to withdraw from it. Such an effort requires that Jews separate the sacred from the profane in their moral existence and, ideally at least, orient themselves toward the sacred. So important was this that the biblical prophets characteristically saw correct moral behavior as more meaningful than required rituals.

Similarly, it is not a Jewish ideal to lead an ascetic life. Abstaining from bodily pleasures, important in some other religions, is not viewed as holy in Judaism.

Jewish efforts to recognize the holy emerge, for example, in prayers and blessings after meals or surviving an illness or for a safe journey and for many other experiences.

Some personal virtues are focused on improving the self.

Study

Jews were seen and see themselves as a "people of the Book." It is Torah that is holy, not a person. There is a distinction between the Torah and Torah. *The Torah* refers to the first five

books of the Hebrew Bible, the sacred text given at Mount
Sinai. *Torah* in general refers to a broader concept of God's
instruction and guidance. As such, the term refers to all of Judaism's wisdom, all the works of Jewish law and all teachings from
all the past until the present moment. As such, Torah continues
as each succeeding generation searches for how Jewish wisdom
can be applied to life. Since Torah embraces all of human
knowledge and moral insights, no area of study is foreign to it.
The knowledge of the world, filtered through Jewish wisdom
and ethical insights, is part of what it means to study. This tradition of embracing knowledge and studying the world is not only
why Jews have made unique and monumentally consequential
spiritual contributions to human civilization but also why Jews
like Einstein and Freud have contributed to the wider sum of
human knowledge.

Jews have always been students, for learning, they believed,
gave them access to the will of God, to the thoughts and observations of the sages. They valued the caress of sacred knowledge.
An important biblical verse, part of the Sh'ma prayer's first para-
graph, notes that in regard to the Bible's commandments, "You
shall teach them diligently to your children" (Deuteronomy 6:7).
In the Mishnah, the particularities of a religious curriculum are
laid out: a child (that is, given the era, a boy) should study the
Bible at age five, the Mishnah at age ten, keep the commandments at age thirteen, and study the Gemara at age fifteen.

Also, the concept of education should not be confused with
the concept of schooling. Jews studied on a regular basis as
adults after they had completed schooling. The Talmud was a
great sea, after all, and mastering its currents required a lifetime
or more. There was a popular Jewish saying: "Make friends of
your books." And it was Rabbi Hillel who cautioned, "Do not say
'When I have leisure I shall study.' Perhaps you will never have
leisure." Learning became a lifelong activity and scholars were
prized in the community.

The systematic history of Jewish persecution was another influence on learning. Jews found themselves sometimes having to leave their homes for faraway places. They therefore learned to prize what was portable. Judaism was centered on a scroll or a book not a Temple. Therefore the Jews could carry their religion wherever they went. Similarly, those who persecuted Jews could take away property and goods. They could not, however, take away what the Jews had learned. And learning was also portable; you could transport your knowledge wherever you went.

For generations before the Haskalah (Jewish Enlightenment) at the beginning of the nineteenth century, Jewish males were literate because reading sacred literature required it. Most people probably were closest to the prayer book, but for those able to do so, it was the study of the Talmud that formed the basis of education. There were times in Jewish history when secular materials supplemented the sacred. Perhaps the most famous was the twelfth and thirteenth century among Spanish Jews. After political emancipation and the emergence of Haskalah, Jews began to study secular subjects, hungry for knowledge that had not generally been available to them.

Self-Control

Self-control involves habitually practicing temperate behavior, being moderate in appetites and emotions. This can mean, for example, drinking in moderation or retaining control over the emotions, not getting too angry or too envious.

Other personal virtues are oriented toward dealing with other people.

Self-Sacrifice

All Jewish virtues find color and depth in stories that illustrate them. And so it is with self-sacrifice. Consider the story of Rabbi

Alexander Goode, an Army chaplain. In January 1943, at age thirty-one, Rabbi Goode was assigned to Greenland to serve as the Jewish chaplain. It was not what he wanted. There was a war raging in Europe, and he wanted to be close to it, to be near the Jews in danger. However, he agreed to his assignment.

Goode was on the freighter *Dorchester* during the first week of February. The ship, old and rusty, was slow-moving. Rabbi Goode was aware of the Nazi submarines patrolling in the North Atlantic, and so the ship's condition troubled him. Still, he found companions with whom to speak. There were three other chaplains on board, the Protestant ministers George L. Fox and Clark V. Poling and the Roman Catholic John P. Washington.

The convoy of ships including the *Dorchester* reached St. Johns, Newfoundland, on February 2. New supplies were taken on, mail was sent, and there was a respite before resuming the voyage. The ships set sail again at 8 p.m.

At 1 a.m. on February 3, a single bell rang, announcing the time. This was simply routine. However, almost immediately after the bell rang, a torpedo hit the *Dorchester* below the water line. There was an order to abandon ship. John Mahoney, dashing to the edge of the ship, suddenly realized he had forgotten the gloves he would desperately need to survive in the icy waters. Mahoney raced back toward his cabin. He met Rabbi Goode, and the rabbi gave his own gloves to Mahoney, assuring him that there was another pair available. Mahoney later learned that not only was there no other pair of gloves, but also Rabbi Goode had earlier given his life preserver to an enlisted seaman who did not have a preserver of his own. The other chaplains had done the same.

There were forty men in John Mahoney's lifeboat. Two survived. Mahoney was one of them, thanks in part to Rabbi Goode's gloves.

Some in the lifeboats reported that they saw the four chaplains linked arm in arm, standing together in self-sacrifice, waiting to die, having given up their own lives to allow others, men they did not know, to live.

Life is sacred in Judaism, and in traditional Judaism Jews are allowed to sacrifice their own lives only to avoid violating a few of the 613 mitzvot. These involve committing murder, accepting a foreign God, and sexual misconduct. In a more modern sense, self-sacrifice does not mean just the literal sacrifice of the living self, but is more expansive and includes giving up what one wants to help another in need. Parents engage continually in self-sacrifice, for example. The sacrifice of personal desires or interests for the well-being of others can be seen as the fulfillment of a duty, or, in the context of this book, as part of a mission.

It should be clear, though, that Jewish law does not mandate that a sacrifice be made. There is an interesting story in the Talmud about the ethical dilemma that the option of self-sacrifice can produce. The story is about two men walking in the desert. One of the men has a pitcher of water. The dilemma is that there is not enough water for them both to drink and survive. And so the man with the water has a choice. He can share the water knowing that both men will die. Or he can refrain from sharing, so that one man will survive while the other dies. One Rabbi, Ben Petura, argued that both should drink the water. But the far-better-known Rabbi Akiva thought the opposite, that survival took precedence over shared death. There is no definite ruling in the Talmud, but Rabbi Akiva's status has meant that his ruling has stood.

Honesty

Honesty is often interpreted as simply telling the truth, wholly and without any misleading implications. But honesty requires judgment. We have to, for example, learn to be honest with ourselves. We have to be analysts not ideologues. Ideologues are experts at ignoring facts. Honest people seek facts out, comprehend them, absorb them into a belief system.

Honesty is more than a personal virtue. Without honesty, there can be no justice. "Thou shall not steal," is one of the Ten Commandments. In biblical times it was an injunction against kidnapping, but in later texts the Rabbis applied the injunction to any theft.

The Rabbis also considered the ways in which a thief could make restitution, as was required. It was, for example, not acceptable simply to offer a payment for the stolen item. The item itself had to be returned, except in the case in which it had been damaged or lost. If a thief had stolen items from many people in so exhaustive a manner so as not to be able to identify the rightful owner of a particular item, the thief was required to undertake some public good. The Rabbis mentioned the possibility of a fountain or garden.

Humility

In some of the more brazen quarters of modernity, humility may be seen as a fault not a virtue. We sometimes see humble people as in need of an injection of self-esteem. We might falsely praise them or fill them with dishonest evaluations of their accomplishments and potential. But being humble does not mean a person lacks self-esteem. Humility is a moral choice, one that, according to Jewish sages, all humans should follow. Indeed, Rabbi Joshua ben Levi concluded that humility was the greatest of the virtues. Humility is not a character flaw in need of repair, but a moral goal that should be eagerly sought.

Humility arises from the self, and the Jewish view of the self puts achievements in perspective. Our selves are not immortal. We all decay. The Rabbis taught that Adam was created as the last of all created beings, not the first. And life's fortunes vary. The economically successful person now may later find financial calamity. The entertainment stars of today may find their hour on the stage has ended. We need, then, to see our own worth and our own importance not as permanent. We need to be humble.

Our abilities might be developed, but we did not give birth to them. They are a part of our creation. We can't, therefore, fully take credit for them. And we don't always understand them. Humans often confuse activity with achievement.

We need honesty about our place in the cosmos. If we are honest, we will be humble, not unmindful of what we have accomplished, but conscious of what we have not, how we were able to become accomplished, including what we owe other people.

For Jews, the dependence on God is reinforced every time a prayer is said. It should be remembered, though, as a companion thought, that the Jewish view of humans doesn't make us simply creatures without skills or will or abilities. We are God's partner. We speak with God. We wrestle with God. We challenge God. The humility is balanced with a healthy sense of our own being.

Cultivating humility produces various worthwhile emotional by-products. Being humble makes people be more prepared, more willing, and more able to engage in honest self-examination. We know ourselves more deeply and more thoroughly. We see areas of weakness, and we can strive for genuine self-improvement, and be able to measure it accurately. Seeing our own selves with honesty, we are less prepared to judge others, even as we are able to appraise others. There are plenty of people whose admiration for humility is under control. We can evaluate them more accurately and understand them more deeply. We will not seek to control them, or anyone else.

We cultivate humility because by doing so we can cultivate all the other moral virtues more easily.

Compassion

Rachmones is the Yiddish word for compassion. The etymology
is important, for the word stems from the same root as the word
for birth. Having compassion is like being a parent to someone.
Compassion is not, of course, exclusively a Jewish virtue. All
good people of whatever faith or faithlessness are compassionate. Indeed, there are many virtues that Jews consider important that are really human virtues. To call them Jewish is simply
to stress the Jewish moral obligation to practice them, to fit
Judaism within the context of being a human being.

Compassion is the emotional capacity to identify with another person's suffering. Being compassionate means being
able to connect some memory or imaginative construct of pain
we had or might have had with the real agony another person
is enduring. But compassion then goes beyond that emotional
identification. It requires that an attempt be made to relieve the
other person's suffering. It means caring for the poor, the sick,
the person with a handicap, the person grieving about a death,
a person overcome by anxiety.

Compassion in Jewish thought is not limited to other Jews.
Compassion is meant for all, and that includes Gentiles

Jewish sacred writing singles out particular people in need
of compassion. These include strangers, widows, and orphans.
The Talmud also stresses not to accuse those who are suffering of being punished for sins they have committed. It should
be added that Rabbis in the Talmud regularly called upon the
suffering themselves to consider if they were being punished
for sins and to engage in self-examination as they suffered.
Evidently, self-criticism was important but criticizing others was
considered unduly cruel.

In keeping with this ideal, it was considered important not to
shame others, to insult them.

From this emphasis on compassion, it might be assumed that
compassion was seen as a boundless virtue. But being compas-

sionate requires a realistic assessment of the other person's situation. To be compassionate is not to be sentimental. If a person does an injustice and then suffers, the person shouldn't be helped out of compassion. The killer in the court who murders his sister shouldn't then be comforted because he has lost a sibling. If compassion prevailed in such cases, there could never be true justice. Compassion properly understood requires a recognition of the reality of the tough side of the world. Such a recognition requires the surrender of being naïve. We shouldn't be compassionate to people who aren't themselves compassionate. Compassion requires us to reject the cruelty of others.

We need to be aware of the dangers in developing a moral temperament as absolute. Believing so intently in the good might become a blindfold blocking off a clear vision of the nastiness that sometimes occurs in the world. Hitler walked the Earth disguised as a human being. Evil can fool us. Morality is only good when it is understood in a complex enough way. Seeing all humans as moral can distort a realistic analysis of some people's depravity and dangerous designs. It can make a person disappointed in people and therefore cynical. Our efforts to do good therefore must be realistic and cover not only the areas where people can do good but also how people can appropriately react to the amoral or immoral behavior of others.

Kindness to Animals

Compassion to humans extends as well to animals. This coheres with the rules of kashrut, of keeping kosher, that stress animals not feeling pain as they die. There is also, for example, an old Jewish custom of not saying to someone wearing a new piece of clothing or an accessory made of leather or fur that they should wear it in good health. The leather or fur came from killing an animal.

The ethical nature of being kind to animals can be seen in the description of a change of diet by Rabbi Joseph Telushkin in his excellent book *A Code of Jewish Ethics, Volume 2: Love Your Neighbor as Yourself.*

Rabbi Telushkin notes in that book that he had always been a meat eater, even recounting his passion for a good steak, hamburgers, or chicken. At various moments, it struck him that it was wrong to kill animals simply to satisfy his own appetites, and he would attempt to stop eating any meat. His grandfather, Rabbi Nissen Telushkin, chided him a bit, observing that the Torah permitted the eating of meat and asked whether he really had to be more compassionate and righteous than the Torah. His grandfather added another argument: Hitler was a vegetarian. (Joseph Telushkin noted that Hitler's vegetarianism was sporadic.) Eventually Joseph realized that he simply lacked the willpower to withstand the lures of a hot dog or hamburger.

It took him several months to research the section on vegetarianism for the second volume of his extraordinary work *A Code of Jewish Ethics*. One day he was staring at the chicken being readied for the Shabbat meal. Rabbi Telushkin realized he could not eat it. His research had taught him the horrific conditions under which chickens are raised (e.g., "most chickens spend their lives confined in an area about the size of a piece of typing paper"). He simply could not eat the chicken knowing what his own research had taught him. Rabbi Telushkin noted that Franz Kafka was once looking at fish at an aquarium in Berlin. Kafka had become a complete vegetarian, extending his refusal to eat meat to include fish. Kafka said to the fish, "Now I can at last look at you in peace. I don't eat you anymore."

Forgiveness

There is a famous distinction in Judaism about what can be forgiven on Yom Kippur, the holiest of Jewish days, the day given over exclusively to atonement. On Yom Kippur, God can forgive sins humans have committed against God, provided we are sincere in our determination not to repeat the sins. But not even God will forgive the sins we have committed against other human beings. We must approach them directly, if that is possible, and ask for their forgiveness. We have to make restitution for the sin, and only then seek forgiveness.

And we are supposed to forgive others if they are sincere in their regret. In doing so, we are imitating God's mercy and compassion. In the Amidah prayer, for example, God is called "the One who forgives abundantly." And there is the Jewish notion that if someone has done you good, let that be seen as great in your eyes, but if someone has done you wrong, that should be seen as less important in your eyes.

Like so many other moral virtues, it is possible to make of forgiveness an easily grasped concept. It is not. Forgiveness can, for example, directly conflict with justice. The struggle between mercy and justice is complex, as we saw in the case of Simon Wiesenthal in the first chapter.

Avoiding Derogatory Speech about Others (*Lashon Hara*)

Lashon hara means "the evil tongue." It involves talking in nasty ways about others. Finding joy in the misfortune of others, seeking out others' purported weaknesses, spreading gossip about others, all these are examples of lashon hara, or related ideas. It should be noted that derogatory speech is true speech, but speech that can embarrass, demean the person, result in financial damage, and so on.

Lashon hara is insidious because it is difficult to make amends for the damages we do to a person's good name. The damage is literally incalculable because we can't chart the chain of gossip that developed from our initial comments.

EXERCISES

We learn lessons in life from all kinds of places. I was an English major in college and an English professor for more than three and a half decades. All of that love of literature started one day when I was thirteen. I was in my small-town library. There may not have been many books, but that didn't matter at the time because I wasn't familiar with the contents of almost any of them. I was wandering the stacks looking for a book to read. Suddenly the librarian told me the library was about to close, and I had to make a choice. I scanned the titles desperately, but none seemed familiar. Then I came upon a book titled *Babbitt* by Sinclair Lewis. I didn't then know that Lewis had been the first American to win the Nobel Prize in literature or that the book was about small-town life. What I recalled was an Abbott and Costello cartoon in which the Costello character had called the Abbott character "Babbitt." Armed with this enormous cultural knowledge, I decided the book would be funny, so I chose it.

That evening I sat down on the couch and began reading. Very soon, on the second page in fact, I put the book down for a second, overwhelmed by the prose. I could not believe that someone just using words could capture so much truth. That one book, not quite but almost the first adult book I had read, led me to a lifetime of reading and learning. Literature led me to ethical questions and dramatic situations. It was a companion to my Jewish learning.

Who influenced you to learn? Were there teachers who changed your life? A family member or friend? A book or movie? How did your ethical education proceed? How did you acquire Jewish teachings to develop your ethical self?

8

LOVE, MARRIAGE, AND FAMILY
IN THE JEWISH TRADITION

In a secular age, marriage is usually defined as a social institution, and not an altogether successful one. Within the Jewish belief system, though, marriage is much more than that. Marriage is a mandate from God as seen in the original creation of Adam and Eve. Marriage is sacred. Marriage is a way for a person to find completion. That is, marriage is much more than a social glue keeping societies together. The marital relationship is part of God's plan for humanity. Indeed, the word for marriage is *kiddushin,* which means "sanctification." One Jewish saying illustrating the importance of the marital relationship is that "marriage takes precedence over the study of the Torah." Marriage between two people is considered analogous to the relationship God has with the Jewish people (illustrated in the "Song of Songs" in the Bible) and between the Sabbath day and the Jewish people (as represented in "Lekhah Dodi," a song meaning "Come My Beloved" that is sung in synagogues at sundown to welcome the Sabbath; while the final verse is sung the congregation stands and turns to the back or toward a door to greet "Queen Shabbat" as she enters).

Judaism teaches that marriage is preferable to celibacy; there is no sense of holiness in remaining unmarried in the Jewish faith. It also teaches that sexuality is good and should be enjoyed.

A marriage, though, does not exist for its own sake. It is a gateway to a wider Godly plan: the creation of a home and family. One principal purpose of a Jewish marriage is to produce Jewish children. A partner in life is needed for people to complete their life purposes, not just to fulfill romantic desires or even to have families. That is part of the reason why marriage of a Jew to another Jew is emphasized. There is, of course, much human drama in the internal struggle between desire and duty. It's not that the two are incompatible but that the former can push aside or disrupt the latter.

The ultimate purpose of a marriage goes beyond providing love and companionship, but that notion of a marital partner completing a self is an important one. A marriage makes a full person. The completed partnership is in the image of God. A partner is not therefore just a partner but a person who can provide sufficient complementarity to allow a person to be a different, better person, to alter and reshape an identity in a positive way, to provide advice, encouragement, and support for personal missions to be discovered and fulfilled. A good marriage provides a person with confidence, a strong sense of self, and through that a resilience to bounce back from adversity.

Marriage rules developed and evolved slowly. Originally, in the Bible a man could have a second wife. This, however, was formally banned among Ashkenazi Jews in the year 1000 by Gershom Me'or Ha-Golah.

In biblical times, the father in a family planned for the marriage of his sons and daughters. Typically the groom paid a dowry to the family for the right to marry a bride, who became his property. By the era of the Second Temple, young women had more of a choice. This is reflected in the Talmud: "A man is forbidden to accept betrothal for his daughter while she is a minor. He must wait until she is of age and says, 'This is the man I choose.'"

There was, unsurprisingly, always much interest in arranging marriages. A popular Jewish saying asserts that "God's occupation is sitting and arranging marriages." If so, it is a tough job, and therefore Judaism allows for divorce.

However difficult, some brave humans ventured into the territory of arranging marriages. The matchmaker (in Hebrew, *shadkhan*) developed from the beginning of Jewish life. Eliezer, Abraham's servant, was the first matchmaker (Genesis 24), choosing Rebekah to marry Abraham's son Isaac. The choice was made because Rebekah was kind and her family had connections to Abraham. The shadkhan was an important figure starting in the Middle Ages. The matchmaker got 2 percent of the dowry—but 3 percent if the couple lived more than ten miles from each other. By more modern times, starting in the nineteenth century, the matchmaker became somewhat of a figure of ridicule. The shadkhan was known to exaggerate and to understate or ignore physical and character flaws.

The tradition of matchmaker did not travel well across the Atlantic when large numbers of Eastern European immigrants arrived starting in the 1880s. The male new American matchmakers developed a sort of uniform: they had beards, wore a derby hat, and, in a not-always-successful attempt to indicate success in the Golden Land, they carried an umbrella.

The system worked like this: the matchmakers, known on the Lower East Side of New York as "Cupids of the Ghetto," located a suitable (or roughly suitable) young man and approached a young woman's family. The mother began the discussion with a detailed list of the prospective bride's extraordinary talents. Maybe she could cook magnificently or enjoyed taking care of young children. If she had the slightest musical talent, this was presented as having great skill, say, at playing the piano. Maybe she had business skills, such as being a stenographer, bookkeeper, and typist. It was common, for example, on the Lower East Side of New York to suggest the woman had *alle drei*, or "all three" of these skills. There was a sort of mathematical ratio the matchmakers assumed. The more skills listed, the less physically attractive. When the parents refrained from bragging about skills, they were suggesting that the young woman was a beauty. The bride's family was of course interested in the bridegroom. What was his family like? Could he support their daughter and any future children? Just how religious was he? The next part of the discussion involved the dowry. This is often thought of as a crude monetary transaction, an exchange of money for marriage approval. But it was not seen like that for the people involved. For the bride's family, the dowry was a source of great pride.

If the discussion went well, it was time for the next step. The matchmaker took the potential bridegroom for a first visit to the prospective bride. The bride's siblings naturally saw how crucial this meeting was and therefore realized they could extract a bribe of their own from their parents and sister. Much candy and gifts exchanged hands. And, at least in the folklore of the Lower East Side, there was another problem.

Sometimes there was a pretty younger sister, someone the visiting gentleman might, Heaven forbid, like more than the would-be bride. Parents, it was said, "suggested" that this younger sister be unable to attend the dinner. Perhaps the family borrowed some silverware. They cleaned. They dressed. And, if all worked out, this dinner, fraught with fears and hopes, eventually led to marriage. Sometimes, though, there were problems. Perhaps the matchmaker didn't receive his fee; he would then break off the marriage. If the man was responsible for the problem, the shadkhan might, for example, find the young woman a more attractive man with more learning or better economic prospects. The shadkhan has, for better or worse, mostly but not completely disappeared from contemporary Jewish life. Still, some contemporary single Jews continue to look for their *bashert* ("destiny" in Yiddish), the person who will make them whole, or, in traditional terms, the person God has chosen for them to meet and marry, the person they are supposed to marry to let them complete their missions. Other Jews have ignored the elusive search for the right person and are looking for any suitable partner.

Some who look depend on family and friends for introductions or meeting someone at a workplace or popular spot such as a club. Others make a more formal effort such as through a Jewish online dating service.

Many of the customs of a Jewish wedding go back to ancient times. Other customs, such as the presentation of a ring to the bride, are more recent. In Talmudic times, a couple was legally wed if any of the following occurred in the presence of at least two witnesses: the man presented a valuable article to a woman, the man presented a written document about the marriage to the woman, or cohabitation (in which case the witnesses remained discreetly outside).

Later elements of the official marriage included the *ketubah*—the legal contract between the marriage partners. Although the idea of a contract emerged from the original notion of the woman as a piece of property, quite early (the first century BCE) the ketubah became a listing of the women's rights in the marriage. While for a long while women remained in an inferior status, the ketubah raised her status. The ketubah, written in Aramaic, is signed by two witnesses prior to the marriage ceremony. In some Reform ceremonies, a certificate of marriage is given to the couple though not read at the wedding ceremony.

Orthodox, Conservative, and a large number of Reform weddings are conducted under a marriage canopy, a chuppah (which means "covering"). This custom originally involved the groom's tent. *Chuppah* originally referred to that tent. But as Jewish life became more difficult, many Jewish men did not have their own home or own room. They often lived with the bride's family. Over time, the practice of having the wedding under a canopy emerged.

The marriage ceremony itself involves an invocation, a betrothal benediction recited over a cup of wine, the ring ceremony, the reading of the ketubah, the Sheva Berakhot, or seven benedictions, recited over a second cup of wine, and, at the ceremony's conclusion, the stepping on a glass by the bridegroom. There is a Talmudic story of a sage who arranged a marriage for his son. The sage observed that the rabbis at the wedding were very joyous. "So he seized a costly goblet worth four hundred zuzim and broke it before them. Thus he made them somber." One interpretation of the glass breaking is that it is a reminder that even in the happiest of moments it is wise to recall the saying that, by tradition, Solomon had put on his ring: "This, too, shall pass." That is, any happiness will not last forever. The wisdom emerges from the opposite as well. In moments of sadness, it is wise to remember that the sadness will pass and happiness will return.

There are many modern additions to that traditional ceremony such as an address by the wedding officiant to the couple. And there are variations by different Jewish groups. In some Orthodox ceremonies the bride walks around the bridegroom as she arrives under the chuppah.

There are many different customs involving weddings. For example, the Belzer Hasidim invited the souls of all their deceased ancestors to the ceremony. Because many believed in the imminent arrival of the Messiah, who would transport ev-

eryone to the Land of Israel, Rabbi Lebi Yitzhak of Berditchev
wrote in wedding invitations he sent out: "The wedding will take
place on [date inserted] at five o'clock in Jerusalem, the holy
city. But if, God forbid, the Messiah will not have come by then,
it will take place in Berditchev."

A *badchen*, or jester, was another wedding custom. The word
badchen came from a verb in the Talmud meaning "to make
people laugh" and "to cheer up." This forerunner to the Jewish
stand-up comedian was popular in Eastern Europe. The badchen kept the wedding guests entertained, telling rhyming jokes
about the marital couple, for example. Unlike the modern-day
comedian, however, the badchen was also a scholar capable of
making involved Talmudic references.

Eliakum Zunser was one of the most famous of these enter-
tainers. He billed himself as Eliakum Badchen. He appeared in
the 1860s. By then, the badchen had transformed into a rude
and coarse entertainer. Eliakum brought the tradition back to
its moral beginnings. He offered ethical maxims, riddles, and
compliments in rhyme as he addressed the bride just as she was
about to go under the chuppah.

As tradition receded, marriage became more complicated in
the modern world. Jewish marriages faced various new hurdles.
Among them, especially in the United States, was that both Jewish men and Jewish women struggled with stereotypes that may
have been absorbed by potential partners. Jewish men (think
of the Woody Allen character in such films as *Annie Hall*) were
seen as neurotic wimps. Other Jewish male stereotypes focused
on being self-absorbed or unathletic. Jewish women were
sometimes stigmatized as JAPs—Jewish American Princesses—
selfish, pampered, spoiled by wealthy and status-seeking parents, whiny, and materialistic like their parents. The stereotype
reflected strains in Jewish social life, as Jews, so recently in the
lower classes, struggled to maintain their new status in higher

echelons of the society. The stereotyping did considerable damage precisely because both Jewish men and women to some extent accepted the stereotypes making both Jewish men and Jewish women more questionable as a future marriage partner.

This stereotyping joined other strains of the post–World War Two era on Jewish marriages. The most prominent challenge to traditional Jewish marriage came from a desire to marry someone not born Jewish.

In Jewish law it is forbidden for a Jew to marry someone who is not Jewish. Indeed, marriage laws traditionally were very precise. A *kohen*, a member of a priestly group within Judaism and by tradition a direct descendant of Moses's brother Aaron through paternal descent, was traditionally not even allowed to marry a convert to Judaism. But modernity has complicated tradition at every turn. Suppose, for example, a Reform Jew who was born to a Jewish father and non-Jewish mother but who identifies as being Jewish and was educated and raised exclusively as Jewish and therefore recognized as Jewish by the Reform movement's patrilineality principle wants to marry a Conservative Jew or Orthodox Jew. Neither movement currently recognizes the patrilineality principle as legally valid, and therefore the marriage is not viewed as a Jewish marriage. An intermarriage was traditionally defined as a marriage between a Jewish person and a Gentile, but, as the example above illustrates, it is no longer even clear what constitutes an intermarriage. It should also be noted that a marriage between a Jew and a convert is not an intermarriage. However, not all movements or rabbis accept the conversions performed by others. But within each movement in the United States when a convert is by the movement's rules allowed to marry a Jew, that is considered an in-marriage.

The Torah's injunction against intermarriage is clear. In regard, for instance, to the seven native Canaanite tribes, Deuteronomy 7:3–4 notes: "You shall not intermarry with them; do not give your daughters to their sons, nor take their daughters for your sons. For they will turn your children from following Me to worship other gods."

That is, the original opposition to intermarriage was in fact a fear of idolatry. It should, however, also be noted that there are many examples of biblical intermarriages, including by Moses, perhaps the most historically important Jew who ever lived. But the prohibition against intermarriage, while not always obeyed, was considered crucial in Jewish history. Intermarriage was seen as reflecting an indifference or even hostility to Judaism, a defiance of the rules and customs of the community and beyond that a threat to its demographic continuity, an understandable but inappropriate reaction to persecution, hatred of Jews, and an inability to rise in the society on the one hand and alluring gestures of welcome and assimilation on the other. After haskalah, the Jewish Enlightenment, and political emancipation in Western Europe, Jews often used intermarriage as a way to escape their history and what some saw as a burdensome identity.

For much of Jewish history, the strictures against intermarriage were powerful. Many families "sat shiva," that is, observed the formal rites associated with mourning the dead, when a child intermarried.

In contemporary America both the number of intermarriages and the acceptance of them have increased greatly. According to the National Jewish Population Survey taken in 1990, there were 720,000 intermarried couples. The rate of intermarriage, which became a national headline, was 52 percent. There has been since then considerable dispute about these and later numbers. It seems reasonable to assume that there are now well over a million intermarried couples in the United States.

While Orthodox and Conservative rabbis are not currently allowed to officiate at an intermarriage, the Reform movement allows rabbis to decide for themselves whether or not they will preside at such marriages and what conditions they might impose on the couple. Both the Reform and Conservative movements have begun active welcoming programs to make the intermarried feel accepted in synagogues and other organizational arms of the movements.

Additionally, other organizations have arisen to assist the intermarried. Here is a self-description used by one principal organization, the Jewish Outreach Institute:

> The Jewish Outreach Institute seeks to insure Jewish continuity. By providing an inclusive Jewish community, JOI believes that children of interfaith families will develop a Jewish identity. Instead of excluding interfaith families from the Jewish community, JOI believes that it is necessary to welcome them and educate them about Judaism.
>
> The past decades have witnessed the growing realization on the part of key institutions of the organized Jewish community that their long-term vitality depends (in no small measure) on how effectively they respond to the forces of assimilation of American Jewry. Most notable among those forces are intermarriage and disconnectedness from Jewish communal institutions. Both those forces have challenged the organized Jewish community to develop strategies of outreach that can engage and connect those segments of the American Jewish population who are currently not at all or only minimally involved in Jewish life.

There are ongoing disputes within the Jewish community about the effectiveness of outreach to the intermarried and therefore how much money, time, and effort should be allocated to preventing intermarriage, encouraging conversion, or welcoming the intermarried. Many opponents of outreach focus on encouraging Jewish children to have a day school education and in other ways have Jewish experiences.

Same-sex marriage and homosexuality itself also are controversial within the American and Israeli Jewish communities. The Orthodox movement in the United States is the only movement that continues to ban same-sex marriages. This is in keeping with the traditional view that homosexuality was a sin. A more contemporary understanding of homosexuality rejects the notion that such acts are in fact sinful. Like the broader American society, there is an increasing acceptance within American Judaism of gays and lesbians and same-sex marriages.

Because marriage is so central an institution in Jewish life, any challenge to it is considered dangerous. The temptation to cheat on one's spouse is considered natural but absolutely necessary to resist. It was in tradition part of the "evil urge," and so Judaism saw in the ability to turn away from its allure, to find the moral restraint necessary to withstand the powerful physical and emotional attractions of someone other than a spouse, the living definition of heroism.

Adultery is condemned in Judaism as a violation not only against one's spouse but against one's entire family, community, and, ultimately, against God. In rabbinic tradition, adultery's definition was expanded to include a person's gazing with desire on a married person. In modern Jewish thought, adultery requires sexual relations not simply sexual desire. The thought is not equal to the deed, however much the thought should be channeled down more appropriate avenues of the mind. Similarly, in Jewish law adultery meant a betrothed or married woman's voluntary sexual relationship with someone who was not her husband or husband-to-be. A married man was forbidden to have relations with a married woman who was not his wife. In modern times, the concept of adultery is applied equally to men and women.

As vital as a marriage was considered, Judaism never explicitly forbade divorce. However, in biblical times a divorce, like marriage and other matters, reflected the belief that a wife was property. Therefore a man could divorce a woman if there was something about her he didn't like and then wrote her a bill of divorcement. (There were minor exceptions to this in which cases the man could never divorce his wife. The exceptions included, for example, if the man had charged that his wife had not been a virgin at the time of the marriage and the charge was later proved false.)

Rabbi Gershom (ca. 960–1030) changed this practice. He altered the Ashkenazic law regarding divorce so that a man could not divorce a woman unless she consented to the divorce. This seeming equality in tradition, however, is partially misleading. For, to this day in Orthodox Judaism a man must provide the bill of divorcement (called a *get*) to his wife. But if the man, for example, cannot be located, the woman remains an *agunah*, a wife who is "tied" to her husband and therefore cannot remarry. Similarly, outside Israel, a man cannot be compelled to give his wife a get. Sometimes this situation becomes very difficult. The Conservative movement has tried to deal with this problem by inserting a clause in the marriage contract saying in case of marital difficulties both partners agree to abide by decisions of a Conservative *bet din*, or religious court. When the husband cannot be located, the bet din invokes the principle of a retroactive annulment, rendering a divorce unnecessary. Since this clause was originally included in the marriage contract, some state courts have ruled that the clause is not legal. Therefore, while the clause is still used in many marriages, in some the couple signs a separate letter saying that the provisions of the marriage contract have been explained to them. This letter is used as a civil document in courts. Because some Conservative rabbis are unsure of the religious status of such a letter, some use other approaches such as retroactive annulment.

The Reform movement does not require the traditional get, allowing instead for a civil divorce to provide acceptable legal permission for the spouses to marry others. Some Reform rabbis nonetheless encourage divorcing couples to obtain a get because otherwise their divorce would not be recognized by Orthodox and Conservative religious courts and future children by either partner in the divorce would be regarded as illegitimate. A marriage is meant, when possible, to produce children, to make a complete family. The Rabbis thought that the biblical injunction to "be fertile and increase" (alternately, "be fruitful and multiply") was the first of the 613 binding commandments.

People first experience a family as children. There are, of course, circumstances in which children are not brought up in families, but the ideal situation is a complete, two-parent family.

Parents have a variety of obligations to their children. Parents are obliged, insofar as they can, to protect their children from harm, to provide schooling, both religious and secular, and an education beyond schooling in moral values by setting an example. One Talmudic Rabbi asserted that a parent's obligation extended to teaching a child a trade. Parents are obliged to provide their children with emotional security and support.

For their part, children find their principal obligation embedded in the Ten Commandments. The fifth commandment, to honor their parents, is meant in part as an aid in a healthier, lengthier life for parents. The notion of "honor" is more complex than it appears. Suppose, for example, a parent wants to teach a child to be a thief. In that case, the child should disobey the parent. That is, honoring a parent is not tantamount to blind obedience.

In the traditional Jewish family, parents had their own distinctive roles. Particularly in American Jewish culture, though, the Jewish mother has received particular attention. Originally,

for Eastern European Jewish immigrants who came to the
United States in large numbers beginning in the 1880s and
lasting for about forty years, the mother was adored, the object
of virtual veneration. Her boundless love, her willingness to
endure any burden if it would help her children, her selfless-
ness, and her kindness were widely acknowledged and adored
by the Jewish immigrants. They marveled at her ability to produce food seemingly from the air, to keep the family together
in times of deprivation.

For example, the comedian Sam Levenson was fond of telling
a story about his "Mama." Mama Levenson's great pride was in
always being ready in case of unexpected guests. In Genesis,
Abraham abandoned a conversation he was having with God in
order to greet guests. This passage led to the Talmudic belief
that to welcome a guest was greater than meeting the Divine
Presence. To be ready, Mama Levenson always had a pot filled
with chicken legs on the stove. (The legs were the cheapest
parts of the chicken; the family was not able to afford the whole
animal.) Then, one day, came the surprise visitors. Uncle Louis
and Aunt Lena showed up unannounced. They brought along
their eleven children. This was a great challenge for Mama. She
quickly realized that she simply did not have enough chicken
legs to feed everyone. Thinking quickly, she called her own children into the apartment's cramped bedroom. She begged them
to say they didn't like chicken and leave the food for the guests.
The children naturally felt sympathy for their mother and readily agreed, and so, at the table, the Levenson children declined
to eat the chicken legs. After the meal's completion, it was time
for dessert. Again, Mama Levenson faced a dilemma because
she didn't have enough dessert. This time, however, she had no
need to consult with her children in the bedroom. Instead, she
stood up at the table and announced, "Now all the children who
wouldn't eat the chicken don't get any dessert."

This extraordinarily positive and heart-warming view of the Jewish mother was about to change. Some people date the change to work done by the anthropologist Margaret Mead, who was studying Jewish life in the shtetl. She interviewed 128 American Jews who had been born in Europe and asked them about their families. Her research reflected a diversity of experiences, but the publications resulting from the study and stories about her work in the popular press led to a new and far less flattering image of the Jewish mother as someone who genuinely loved her children but showed that love in inappropriate ways such as instilling guilt, smothering them emotionally, and complaining about the sacrifices she had to make on their behalf. The negative stereotype of the Jewish mother then grew to include a woman who manipulated her children in an attempt to control them, who interfered in her children's lives into adulthood. This unflattering portrait, popular especially in the 1960s and beyond, slowly has begun to recede from American media.

Beyond parents, a child's family life also includes siblings. Sibling rivalry was, of course, part of family life, but, as with parents, the ideal family included an unbreakable bond among the siblings. One tale of such fervent loyalty can be found in the story of a sister's bravery. This true story took place at a time in Russia when young Jewish boys were kidnapped and sent to the Russian army. The conscription began in 1827 when boys were drafted at age twelve. The specific purpose was to grab Jewish boys prior to their bar mitzvah and so deprive them of a Jewish identity. Later, Jewish boys were taken as early as age eight and given military and non-Jewish religious training. They entered the military at age eighteen for many years of obligatory service.

This story is about a boy who did not return home from religious school. It was a winter's night, and his parents and sister were deeply worried. The agitated family eventually located one of the boy's classmates who told of the boy's capture.

The sister learned where the boys were being held. It was in a camp just a few miles from the village where the family lived. The parents approached the town's leaders, but no one could offer help. The family, it seemed, would just have to accept that their boy was gone.

The Jewish holiday of Simchat Torah was nearing. (This holy day, literally meaning "Rejoicing with the Torah," marked the transition of the weekly portion of Torah readings with the end of the Torah and the endless cycle of beginning to read it again.) The sister came up with a plan. She had food and a bottle of vodka for the guards and then got into her wagon and drove to the camp. A sentry approached her. The sister did a curtsy and said she wanted to give her brother a present for Simchat Torah. The sentry seemed confused until she handed him a honey cake.

She was grateful the guard had not looked in her bag.

He said she could enter but not stay longer than a half-hour. She found her brother and told him that at the bottom of the bag he would find a dress and a girl's shoes and hat. She told him to put the girl's clothing on, wait for ten minutes after she left, and walk out of the camp. She told him the guard would think she was leaving.

The girl left, watching until the sentry was busy, and, as he turned away, she sneaked out of the camp. Soon her brother came marching along the road, walking very slowly in his new dress. The brother and sister arrived home safely.

The entire family eventually escaped Russia and came to the United States.

Children grow up, marry, and start their own family, and the cycle, like the Torah readings, continues. Being a good Jewish parent means, first of all, being a good parent. It therefore means giving children the confidence and support to find their way in the world, to provide the child with realistic confidence. It means spending time listening to the child. Being a good Jewish parent also means being a good Jew. That requires making Judaism appealing to children and making sure they learn about being Jewish.

No one is a perfect parent or marital partner. But the survival of the Jewish family depends on understanding what is at stake, in finding the right role models, and in seeking to approximate perfection.

EXERCISE

It is worthwhile to see some of the Jewish romantic movies that shaped American Jews' self-perception, including stereotypes. Here is a list of a few of the movies about romance and American Jewish life that were important:

Marjorie Morningstar (1958), based on Herman Wouk's popular novel, about a young woman's coming of age and her romance with an older Jewish entertainer.

A *Majority of One* (1961) starred Rosalind Russell and Alec Guinness as an older Jewish widow and Japanese widower struggling with tolerance and love.

Funny Girl (1968) starred Barbra Streisand as the incomparable Jewish entertainer Fanny Brice.

No Way to Treat a Lady (1968) is the story of a Jewish detective tracking down Rod Steiger as a serial killer. The film prominently includes a classic stereotype of a Jewish mother.

Goodbye, Columbus (1969), based on Philip Roth's novella, is one the early works accused of Jewish stereotyping.

The Heartbreak Kid (1972) concerns the story of a Jewish male breaking up his Jewish marriage to be with a blonde Gentile beauty.

The Way We Were (1973) was about Streisand as a Jewish radical romancing Robert Redford as a handsome Gentile writer.

Annie Hall (1977) is Woody Allen's classic New York film about a Jewish man and a Midwestern woman with a very non-Jewish family.

Add to this list with more contemporary movies you have seen.

9

"DO NOT SEPARATE YOURSELF FROM THE COMMUNITY"

Abba Kovner was a Lithuanian resistance fighter during the Second World War. He later moved to Israel, where he became a poet. After his arrival in Israel, he remained bitter, thinking of his parents and friends who had been killed by the Nazis, feeling alienated and alone. He joined a kibbutz and tried to settle down.

One day a man tugged at his sleeve asking the new Israeli to join nine other people to form a minyan, the ten people needed for prayer to proceed. Suddenly, as he prayed, he felt needed, part of the Jewish community. He finally belonged somewhere.

Many years later the Museum of the Diaspora was being built in Tel Aviv, and Kovner had an idea. He designed a corner that he termed "The Minyan." As he told the story, Kovner thought he would have wax figures representing the wide variety of Jewish communities praying together. He wanted to illustrate that they had a spiritual need for each other and that as they prayed together they formed one united community.

As the museum was about to open, someone noticed with a panic that there were only nine wax figures, when the whole

Jewish world knew ten people were needed for the minyan.
Kovner was approached with the emergency. He said the nine
figures were correct. There was a missing person. That missing
person was a call to each visitor, a request to join the minyan, a
statement that Jewish religious life couldn't go on without the
viewer joining the community.

Kehillah is the Hebrew word for community, the organized groups, organizations, and neighborhoods and other
geographical entities that promote Jewish religious practices,
provide mutual help, offer support, and so on. The term also
can be understood as meaning all the Jewish people conceived
of metaphorically as sharing a communal relationship. The
notion of community is crucial to the Jewish belief system.
There is a Yiddish expression that it's even good not to be
alone in Heaven. A community is vital to provide help at crucial moments. These might be physical crises. The help might
be needed at moments of emotional distress, such as a time
of death. Communities, though, have even a deeper purpose.
They support the ethical teachings of the family. They serve
as a reminder to do good. Ultimately, they provide part of a
person's identity. We are who we are, in part, by where we
belong. Our family helps define us. So do our friends. And so
does the community where we live. The Jewish community is
crucial in providing purpose and definition to an individual's
Jewish identity.

The organizational units of the community start with family,
the unity of a man and a woman that may produce children.
The family is part of the wider community, the most ancient
of which is the clan. In Genesis 2:18, there is an admonition
by God: "It is not good for man to be alone." Judaism is not a
religion that admires hermits or isolated spiritual seekers. Soli-
tude is not a religious virtue. Rather, there is within Judaism a
perceived social need that humans have. They also have ethical
obligations best performed in concert with other people. Com-

munity is an organizing principle of life. Religion does not just involve personal redemption. Therefore, as Ethics of the Fathers admonishes, "Do not separate yourself from the community." It is crucial to participate in society. Doing so is a vital part of both a personal and communal Jewish identity. Such participation is part of undertaking missions in Jewish life. The communal existence of individual Jews is driven by an ethical outlook. In this case, the communal obligations promote social values.

SOCIAL VIRTUES AND OBLIGATIONS

Kindness

The biblical prophets saw acts of being kind as fulfilling God's will. Hosea 6:6 quotes God: "For it is kindness that I desire and not sacrifice." That is, basic rituals were superseded by ethical acts. Similarly, Micah 6:8 charts Godly demands as including being just, walking humbly with God, and engaging in acts of loving-kindness.

There are many stories told about the Jewish sages, including Rabbi Israel Salanter (1810–1883), the founder of the Musar movement, which emphasized Jewish ethics.

This story involves the most sacred of Jewish holy days, Yom Kippur. Rabbi Salanter's synagogue was filled with people waiting to start the Kol Nidre prayer, which is recited before the beginning of the evening service on Yom Kippur. But everyone realized that Rabbi Salanter could not be found. Someone was sent to the rabbi's house, but he was not at home. Congregants joined together, concerned because surely their rabbi would not miss this crucial service on purpose.

A long search was undertaken, and finally the congregants found the rabbi. He was in a tiny, dimly lit home in the poorest section of the town. The rabbi was rocking a baby while singing a religious song.

Shocked, one of the congregants said to the rabbi, "What are you doing here?"

The rabbi spoke up with his answer. "I was on my way to the synagogue when I passed this house and heard a baby's cries. I supposed the family had gone to pray and left the baby alone. So I went in to take care of the child."

Acts of kindness are repaid with gratitude and in other ways as well. Consider the case of Rabbi Henry Cohen (1863–1952), who became well-known in Texas especially for his work on behalf of prisoners of all faiths. Each morning on his shirt cuff he wrote the names of those who needed help, trying to provide that assistance by the evening.

One day, he heard the story of a man named Sidney Porter and began to investigate. Rabbi Cohen determined the man was innocent and went directly to the governor with a request that Porter be freed.

Rabbi Cohen was in his study several months later when there was a knock at the door. As the rabbi opened the door, he saw a man holding a suitcase.

"Are you Rabbi Cohen?"

"I am," the rabbi responded to the stranger.

"I am Sidney Porter, the man you got out of jail. I can't tell you how grateful I am. I can't pay you for your help now, but I'm a writer, and I'll do what I can to help your people."

Years later, Rabbi Cohen read a story concerning an innocent man in jail who had been freed with the help of a rabbi. The story was written by Sidney Porter under his pen name: O. Henry.

Loving Your Neighbor

Leviticus 19:18 includes the most famous injunction about caring for those around us: "Love thy neighbor as thyself." The moral command sounds good, but it is not immediately obvious what it means or how it can be put into practice. For example, what can it mean if there is a direct command to "love" anyone, whether a neighbor or anyone else? Love is personal, emotional, spontaneous. How can it be a moral requirement, an obligation? It is difficult enough to love those we feel we should love much less those among our neighbors we don't even know.

The "love" in the Bible is a guide to moral action. It is a reminder of Hillel that we not do to others what we would not like done to ourselves. It is a reminder of Buber that the surest path to the self is in a human, caring relationship with the other, at least so long as the other acts morally toward us. In context, the line in the Bible is really a call not to seek revenge for being wronged. The "love" here is not about feelings but about ethical behavior.

The prompting of ethical action certainly helps others, but it helps us as well by providing a perspective on the nature of the self we possess. If we act ethically toward others, if we, for example, don't bear a grudge, we help the person against whom we might otherwise feel entitled to mistreat because he mistreated us. By not doing so, however, we help him but we also have the right to call ourselves good for refraining from such behavior. That good behavior shapes our self-understanding and our entire character. That is, the way we behave toward others has the effect of defining our character, of defining both the way others see us and the way we see ourselves. We are our neighbor.

There is an interesting problem in the Talmud. A person has two neighbors in trouble. One neighbor, who is an enemy, is trying to put a heavy load of goods on his animal. Another neighbor, this one a friend, is trying to remove a heavy load of goods from an animal. The Talmud puts the question in this way: Which neighbor should be helped? The answer at first seems simple. We should help the neighbor remove the heavy load not because he is a friend but because in that case both the person and the animal are suffering. But the conclusion reached is the opposite. We should, in fact, help our enemy because by doing so we might transform an enemy into a friend and that takes precedence over simply one friend helping another.

Charity

The well-known British Jewish philanthropist Sir Moses Montefiore (1784–1885) was one of the wealthiest people in the world. A curious person approached him and asked him how much he was worth.

"I am worth forty thousand pounds," Montefiore replied.

The questioner was astonished. "I thought you were worth millions."

The philanthropist smiled. "I do possess millions. But you asked me how much I am worth, and since forty thousand pounds represents the sum I distributed during the last year to various charitable institutions, I regard this sum as the barometer of my true worth. For it is not how much a person possesses, but how much he is willing to share with the less fortunate that determines his actual worth."

Tzedakah, or charity, originally meant the same as justice. It involved righteous behavior. However, by the time of the Talmud the concept developed into a more recognizable modern form meaning to aid the poor. Generally, this meant providing monetary assistance.

But it should not be entirely enjoyable to give charity. The Rabbis feared the charitable person deriving great satisfaction from the giving would be rooting for poverty to never end.

The Rabbis fully grasped that there were thieves and even beggars who pretended that they were poor so as to swindle money from good people. Some "lame" and "blind" needy could walk and see. But the Rabbis also looked down on those who were genuinely needy and did not take help. Of course, there was an emphasis on self-reliance, on accepting the reality of one's situation, but in difficult circumstances the poor were encouraged to seek and accept help. There is a Yiddish saying that a person did not die of hunger but of being too proud to seek help. The Rabbis encouraged people to give one-tenth of their income to charity when such charity was required. However, the Rabbis noted the danger of giving too much to charity because of the ensuing danger that the giver could then become poor as well.

The most famous statement in Jewish literature about charity comes from Maimonides, who developed a list of eight degrees of charity in descending order. But the list is more dramatic if it is presented in its opposite order. Therefore, from the least worthwhile giver to the best, here is the list developed by the greatest medieval Jewish thinker:

1. A person gives to charity, but is saddened when giving.
2. A person is appropriately glad when giving but gives an insufficient amount.
3. A person gives, but only when a poor person asks for help.
4. A person gives without having to be asked, but the money is given directly to the person so that both the giver and receiver know who is involved in the transaction.
5. The donor does not know who gets the gift but the recipient does.
6. The receiver does not know who provided the money, but the donor knows who received it. (In this case, Maimonides has the donor throwing the money into the recipient's house.)
7. The donor gives money anonymously to a charity fund that distributes the money to a needy person. Neither the giver nor the receiver knows the identity of the other. Many

people incorrectly identify this stage as the highest, but there is a higher one yet.

8. The highest form of charity is the gift that prevents the receiver from becoming poor, such as by providing a job or giving money during a difficult part of the person's life. This is the highest form of charity because it prevents poverty from developing.

Additionally, there are many famous Jewish sayings and proverbs about charity. These include:

Charity is equal to all the other commandments combined.
The person who is generous to the poor makes a loan to the Lord.
Do not humiliate beggars; God stands beside them.

Benevolence

Benevolence involves a person, building on a good character, doing good deeds. Unlike charity, benevolence is not aimed just at the poor but at all people even including the wealthy, and it is not just about providing money but providing personal help such as by a kind word or direct nonfinancial assistance. Benevolence, unlike charity, is not even aimed just at the living. A person can be benevolent, for example, by reciting prayers in memory of those no longer alive.

The act of *bikur cholim*, visiting the sick, is a paradigm of benevolent action. But visiting the sick does not refer simply to an occasional meeting with someone who is ill. In its fullest meaning, visiting the sick refers to taking care of those who are ill and, to the extent possible, aiding in their recovery. The focus of concern is on the sick person not the feelings of the visitor. Therefore it is clear in Jewish law that the visits should be at the times most convenient for the sick person and not to extend the visit so as to make the sick person tired. Not every sick person should be visited. For example, a benevolent person should not visit a sick enemy because the ill person may see *schadenfreude* in the visit—that is, the sick person may think the visitor derives pleasure from seeing the enemy's suffering.

Comforting those who are in mourning is another example of benevolent behavior. Similarly, so is attending a funeral and accompanying the deceased to the graveside. Other examples of benevolence include offering kind greetings, lending needed materials when they are needed, being hospitable to guests in one's house, among many other possibilities.

Justice

Justice involves perceiving and understanding the difference between right and wrong, dispensing what is just to people, and treating all people and situations with equality. Justice is fairness.

God's justice is tempered with mercy and mercy with justice. The two are companion concepts, and both are God's attributes.

In a legal sense, justice involves deciding between two conflicting claims. In a criminal case, for example, the conflicting claims are between society and the individual criminal. The problems of retributive justice, punishment for those who are in violation of social laws, are clear in the complicated efforts to have a fair legal system. As a matter of self-defense, societies deny the rights of those who hurt or prey on others. But an individual also has rights, and so a just society cannot provide punishment that exceeds the crime committed by the individual.

People are obliged to be just to others. Employers must provide fair wages for their workers, listen with care to any complaints they may have, and provide their wages in a timely

way. People who own shops must charge a fair price. Any
weights and measures must be accurate. A person cannot take
advantage of another person who is helpless. As the Bible
notes, "thou shalt not curse the deaf, nor put a stumbling block
before the blind" (Leviticus 19:14). That is, if a person puts an
obstacle in the path of a blind person, the guilty person has
committed two offenses. One is to force the blind person to
fall. But the other is simply to have placed the obstacle at all.
Blindness here is used as a metaphor for any innocent person
who should not be deceived in any way.

Indeed, there is an emphasis in Judaism in not just obeying
the law but in going beyond it to provide justice. The going beyond is itself built into the law.

In a broader sense, justice involves fairness and can refer to
an individual, family, people in society, or society as a whole.
Slavery was an injustice, since it involved holding people and
treating them cruelly. The Jewish people have always emphasized being free of political restraints. As the German Jewish
poet Heinrich Heine wrote, "Since the Exodus, freedom has
always spoken with a Hebrew accent." Social justice involves
distributive justice—that is, that in a society the power and resources are fairly distributed. This notion of fairness includes a
special concern for those who are the weakest and the poorest.
It is an ethical obligation to reach out to them. There is therefore a connection between justice and charity.

Medical Ethics and Bioethics

There are a whole variety of current subjects generally
grouped under the subject heading "medical ethics" or "bioethics" that Judaism, like society itself, must confront. These subjects include abortion, artificial insemination, autopsies, birth
control, eugenics, euthanasia, and transplants, among others.

The relatively new subjects have deep roots in Jewish thought. They have come about primarily because of the unprecedented explosion of new knowledge and procedures in medicine. This new medical world has brought with it new ethical issues. Given the legal and medical complexities of these issues, and the sometimes widely divergent interpretations, it is not possible to define a single Jewish position. There are some principles that might be derived from Jewish teachings: (1) the life of every innocent human being is valuable; (2) therefore, life should be preserved when possible through, for example, the practices associated with good health; (3) the religious obligation is to, when possible, have children; (4) marriage is sacred; (5) the suffering or pain of innocent people should be alleviated as much as possible; and (6) the dead should be fully respected.

The application of such principles to real situations continues to be inexact. Consider the extremely controversial subject of abortion. Jewish religious authorities don't have a single response to the question of abortion. Generally, life is viewed as having supreme value. Additionally, a mother's life takes precedence over an unborn infant if it threatens her life. However, suppose the unborn infant does not threaten a mother's life, but threatens her health. Or suppose the unborn infant is known or suspected to have some severe abnormality. The performing of an abortion in these cases divides Jewish legal authorities.

To complicate these matters, questions of medical ethics and bioethics are leading to changes in social attitudes. Besides abortion, for example, the evolution of homosexual rights has expanded considerably in the last half-century. Traditional Judaism and contemporary Orthodox Judaism view homosexual acts as abhorrent. Contemporary non-Orthodox Jews, however, have increasingly accepted gay rights, including gay marriage.

It is these medical and social issues that will continue to provide the source of argument and friction. Perhaps this will even be in an accelerated manner because medical knowledge and social attitudes are changing so quickly about so many subjects.

Judaism and Other Religions

Because Judaism does not require Gentiles to become Jewish in order to achieve salvation, there is no urgent need to convince others to become Jewish. This fact, in theory at least, allows for religious tolerance.

Additionally, contemporary life has become much more secular. A larger percentage of Americans than ever do not consider themselves attached to a particular religion. Some of these people are secular, while others consider themselves spiritual (i.e., believing in God) but not religious (i.e., belonging to a formal organization). In a secular world there is by definition less competition among religions as well as more of a sense that the religious are in a group separate from the secular or simply spiritual members of a society. This situation inevitably draws religions together in common cause. This fact, too, makes all religions in the United States, at least in theory, more tolerant of each other.

This theoretical tolerance and whatever real-life counterpart exists sometimes have the effect of blurring differences among religions. There may be, as neuroscientists suggest, a common underlying moral attitude covered over with a cultural layer of specific religions, and it may be comforting to many, but, however similar humans are underneath and however comforting is the view that all religions are fundamentally the same, it is not the case that all religions ultimately have the same beliefs. This is not to say, however, that underneath the differences, religions undertake the same sort of search, ask many of the same sort of questions, and rely on some fundamental cosmic force, some sacred force, to ground all human beings.

Judaism and Christianity, at least in their mainstream versions, have basically different views about many subjects. The most basic Jewish view of God is that God is a single entity, not, as Trinitarian Christians believe, constituting three parts. For Jews, the Messiah who will usher in an era of peace has not yet come to Earth. For Christians, God the Son appeared on Earth as the Messiah. Christianity believes humans are born in sin and need redemption through Jesus. Jews believe humans are neither good nor bad but have the necessary free will to choose.

Ultimately, the adherent of any belief system has a limited number of options when they consider their relationship to adherents to any other belief system. These options, in terms specifically applied to Judaism, are: (1) Judaism is the one true religion and belief system and all other religions and belief systems are false. Medieval Jewish thinkers generally held this position. This view has generally been dismissed. The value of other religions is more obvious. Many Jews, as do adherents of other religions, see a commonality at the heart of a religious quest even if specific beliefs differ. (2) All religions have the same truth value. This view is that different religions constitute different paths up the same mountain. (It might be added that from a secularist's point of view the religions have the same value, not of truth but of falsity.) The problem with religious relativism is at least twofold. In real life, adherents need a reason to continue affiliating with their religion. They have to see some insight it offers that differentiates it from other belief systems in a positive way. And secondly it is obvious that religions contain principles that are in direct contradiction with principles of some other religions. They can't, that is, both be correct. (3) Other belief systems contain some truths, but Judaism contains more truths than other belief systems. Note that such an assertion can be made about atheists or adherents of other religions as well. The key factor becomes one of tolerance. That is, Judaism, for example, does not believe that followers of other faiths are in any way denied entrance to Heaven. And Judaism can affirm that Jews can learn from studying other religions.

EXERCISES

When I was a child, I went to a local luncheonette to buy an ice cream cone. It cost ten cents, and a dime was all the money I had. While I waited to buy the cone, a slightly older boy in front of me ordered a cone as well, but with sprinkles. The sprinkles sounded very attractive to me, and I asked about them. The owner told me the sprinkles cost an extra penny. I was instantly unhappy because I did not have the penny. Then the older boy, who was still standing off to one side, offered one of his pennies. I got the cone with sprinkles. I didn't know the boy's name, and then suddenly he was gone. I remember his kindness to this day, and, when I can, I try to help people out thinking of him.

Can you recall people who were kind to you and how they affected your life?

My wife, Sharon, volunteers each week. For many years now, she has visited one hospital or another every Sunday. She does it as a tribute to her father, who died when she was young, and to my mother. She has often said that people need to know that those outside the hospital still care about them. Sharon reads them stories and listens to tales they tell of their own lives, of their participation in war, of their families and friends. Sharon thinks these people carry and convey a special wisdom.

Consider joining with a group or on your own visiting a person at home or in a hospital, reaching out to the lonely and the ill.

Jews and Christians have, at least since the post–World War Two era, gotten along very well in the United States. Consider in your life how Jews and Christians have helped each other. Here's an example in my life. I am very close friends with Michael Fitzpatrick, a New York state assemblyman. Mike and I met in the 1980s when we both worked for the same U.S. member of Congress. Mike became very interested in the political activities in which I was engaged on behalf of Israel and Jews trying to emigrate from what was then the Soviet Union. One of those activities involved working with the late Lynn Singer, then executive director of the Long Island Committee for Soviet Jewry. Each Tisha B'av (a Jewish holy day commemorating the destruction of both the First and Second Temples, which both occurred on the ninth day of the month of Av), the committee held a vigil in front of the gates at a country estate in Glen Cove on Long Island. The Soviet delegation to the United Nations rented the estate.

Mike and I had a tradition. Before each Tisha B'av we'd go to a kosher delicatessen and then later go over to the vigil. One year Mike and I were at the vigil. A police officer came over to Lynn and told her that there was a credible bomb threat. The police recommended that we leave. I asked Lynn what she planned to do, and she said it was important to stay despite the potential danger. I told Mike, "I'm going to stay, but this isn't your fight." I told him to go a couple of miles away, and we would meet later.

Mike stared at me and said, "This *is* my fight. I'm staying." And he did.

10

DEATH AND THE AFTERLIFE

A learned rabbi and a taxi driver arrive at Heaven's gate together. There is an angel there to greet them. The angel looks at each of their life records and sends the taxi driver immediately through on into Heaven. The rabbi, though, has to wait. The rabbi is indignant. "I'm a scholar," he yells at the angel. "He was a wild driver who went all over the road. Why did you let him in while I have to wait out here?" The angel pauses and says, "You gave boring sermons and put people to sleep. When that crazy taxi driver had passengers on the road, believe me they prayed."

Sometimes we joke about what makes us anxious, and few subjects provoke as much anxiety as impending death. In discussing the subject, it is wise to invoke Heinrich Heine's observation before discussing the finality of life. Heine wrote, "If you reflect on death, you're already half dead." This fits well with the Jewish emphasis on life, on savoring both the sweetness and pain of existence, on refraining from embracing thoughts of death and the afterlife while neglecting thoughts about this life. We should not, on this account, so look forward to the bright colors of an afterlife even if we see our earthly existence as

being in black and white. Neither should we let depression or
tragedy make death attractive. A graveyard's false gold has lured
many sad people.

There are many stories about the deaths of famous Jews.
Consider the case of Maimonides, the greatest Jewish thinker
of the Middle Ages. The prominent physician and scholar had
as a last wish to be buried in the Land of Israel. His coffin was
accompanied to the Holy Land. Once the body was there, another problem had to be faced. Where exactly would the sage
be buried? Maimonides had not left specific instructions as to
the precise final resting place. Jews from various communities
then entered into a bitter argument, each group claiming its
superiority as an appropriate burial site. Those who came from
Jerusalem said that their city was the spiritual capital of the Jewish people and therefore the most appropriate spot for this great
Jewish spiritual leader. Those who came from Hebron claimed
that Maimonides should be buried in their town because that
was where the patriarchs of the Jewish people were buried.
Eventually, all those fighting realized that in their loud dispute
they were insulting the memory of Maimonides. Eventually, a
strange compromise was reached. The disputants concluded
that the camel carrying the coffin would be allowed to wander
freely around the country going wherever it wished to walk.
Wherever the camel chose to kneel, that would be the spot
chosen to be the great scholar's final resting place. The camel
wandered for several days until it arrived in Tiberias, and it
was there that the camel came to rest. And so Maimonides was
buried in Tiberias.

Other stories focused on who will get admitted to the World
to Come. There is a story, for example, about the biblical
prophet Elijah. A rabbi once approached the prophet and
asked Elijah to point out some people wandering around in the
marketplace who were going to be admitted to the World to

Come after death. Elijah agreed to the request. He then sur-
veyed the various people wandering around and finally pointed
at two jesters. The rabbi was surprised. The jesters were not
well known for their religious knowledge or the fervor of their
religious practices. Curious, the rabbi asked the prophet why
these two would be chosen. Elijah responded that it was the
jesters' job to bring joy, happiness, and a moment of relief for
those in distress, and such an important job merited a place in
the World to Come.

Because of Judaism's emphasis on earthly existence, some
people conclude that Jewish thinkers have not had a lot to say
about what happens after death, but that assertion is incorrect.
Medieval Jewish thinkers especially thought about the question
a lot and had many observations that are not widely known.

The Jewish attitude toward death is one of respect and real-
ism. It combines defiance but also acceptance.

There is an old Jewish saying that for the ignorant old age is
like winter, but for the learned it is harvest time. This reflects
the notion of the accumulation of lifelong study and learning as
imbuing some of the elderly with the time and ability to reflect
both on their life and on human existence. The saying is an argument for continuing to read, think, study, and perhaps even
write throughout one's life. America may worship youth, but Judaism equally praises the old. And, anyone, old and young alike,
who studies Judaism learns the commandment to choose life,
to find it precious, and not to look forward to death. As Woody
Allen put it, "I don't want to achieve immortality through my
work. I want to achieve it through not dying."

The sense of approaching death has led to a traditional con-
fession on the deathbed: "I admit before You, God, my God
and God of my ancestors, that my cure and my death are in
Your hands. May it be Your will that You heal me with a complete healing. And if I die, may my death be an atonement for

the sins, transgressions, and violations which I have sinned, transgressed, and violated before You. And set my portion in the Garden of Eden, and let me merit the world to come reserved for the righteous. Hear O Israel, the Lord our God, the Lord is One."

It is important for those who continue living to react to death appropriately. As the Yiddish saying puts it, "the only truly dead are those who have been forgotten." It is telling that on Purim, which commemorates the triumph of Queen Esther and the defeat of the evil Haman, there is a tradition that continues to the present. On that day, the Book of Esther is read. Each time Haman's name is mentioned, those listening to the reading use a noisemaker called a grogger. The loud noise blots out the sound of Haman's name.

The lesson of this is that honorable and good people deserve to have their name recalled and not overwhelmed by noise. Recalling the dead is one way to preserve them.

Excessive mourning is frowned upon in Jewish life. Even while experiencing the darkness of someone's death we look for light. This is well expressed by the Holocaust survivor and Nobel Peace Prize–winning author Elie Wiesel: "Every death leaves a scar, and every time a child laughs it starts healing."

Taking care of the dead is considered a great mitzvah because the dead cannot return the favor. Ancient Jews were buried in expensive clothes. This led the poor to be embarrassed if they could not afford the garments worn by the wealthy. A change came because Gamaliel, a leading religious authority in the first century CE, put in his will that despite his wealth and status he wished to be buried in linen shrouds, that is inexpensive material. This one act had a major influence allowing poor families the ability to avoid spending all their money on burial clothing.

Traditional Jews still tear a piece of clothing prior to the funeral of close relatives. Many Jews observe a seven-day period of mourning. Tradition called for them to sit on stools placed close to the ground for this period (hence the practice was called "sitting shiva," with "shiva" referring to the seven-day period. Jewish eschatology, its theory of the end of the world, has emphasized the following steps: (1) the Messiah will appear on Earth to usher in a long era of peace and happiness; and (2) the dead will be resurrected. Their souls, until then having resided in Heaven, will be reunited with the bodies.

Kafka wrote, "The meaning of life is that it stops." But traditional Judaism does not believe that. Instead, traditional Judaism believes in the World to Come, of a life after death. In most modern versions, the soul exists apart from the deceased body. For many centuries, and among the more traditional still, Jews believed in the ultimate resurrection of the body.

There are various biblical passages that suggest that at death all humans go to a region for the dead. Although various names for this region are used, the most significant one is sheol. All humans are equal; the powerful and the powerless, the rich and the poor, everyone is alike in going to sheol, a place where, according to some biblical passages, there is no human consciousness. Other biblical passages portray God as taking some humans from sheol to bring them closer.

There are a variety of views in later Jewish literature. Heaven, *shamayyim* in Hebrew, refers to the sky or is used as a name for God. *Paradise* (a Persian word meaning "orchard") isn't included in the Hebrew vocabulary. Instead the World to Come is referred to as Gan Eden, or the Garden of Eden. The standard view is that in Gan Eden our souls are close to God. A more subtle Jewish concept was that the souls of good people grow spiritually even in Heaven, reaching an ever-deeper understanding and appreciation of God and drawing ever closer.

Gehinnom, or Hell, is also discussed by the Rabbis in the Talmud. It is possible to conceive of Hell as a place of punishment for sins. But the more widespread Jewish view is that a wicked person's soul is extinguished, depriving the person of the joy of being close to God. A less thoroughly evil person might be very far from God in the afterlife. This generally medieval notion is rarely discussed in modern Judaism, for better or worse, for it does carry with it a sense of justice, a distinction between a good person and a bad one.

But while contemplation of the precise destination of our souls, like other notions involving death such as contacting the departed or reincarnation, might be interesting, for Judaism, the overwhelming emphasis is on leading moral lives on Earth and trusting in God to take care of what happens afterward.

Of course, many modern Jews do not believe in any kind of an afterlife, seeing death as permanent and without a second act for life. For them, the dead live on through their good deeds, through memories of them by the living, through their children, and through all they did in their lives.

All that can be finally said about this realm is that we can't understand it on Earth, but we can prepare in some way by maintaining a relationship with God and acquiring knowledge, especially knowledge about justice and morality.

There can be constructed complex theories of the afterlife compatible with Judaism and modern science. Here is one such theory:

The human mind can be understood as continuing to exist after physical death in the Mind of God as an existing reality with a continuing life of its own.

A "mind" consists of the current series of mental activities humans have at any given moment and as the collected history of all the mental activities both conscious and unconscious that the mind has ever had. Mental activities include, for example, thinking, reasoning, daydreaming, and planning. These mental activities result in ideas, thoughts, concepts, theories, beliefs, and so on.

Our cumulative collection of previous mental activities exists in two places. Our memory is the first place where our collected past mental activities exist. The memory is an imperfect residence for those past mental activities. We recall some; we misremember others; and we don't remember many, if any, unconscious activities. Besides our memory, our past mental activities also exist in the Mind of God, and it is there that these collected mental activities of a lifetime form the basis of the mind in the afterlife.

Consider when we pray silently. Some idea or thought such as a plea for compassion or protection or a traditionally uttered group of words forms in our mind. We direct this mental activity toward God. God receives those prayers. Just as the prayer leaves our mind, God receives those prayers in an infinite Mind. That part of God that humans can understand as being comparable to the human mind is most easily comprehended as a Mind, whatever in reality it should be called. With an infinite Mind, God retains all the communications from humans, even after we physically die. The idea of a mind's afterlife in the Mind of God, then, is that a human mind continues to exist in the Mind of God after death.

The idea of the human mind existing in the afterlife goes back to the Greeks and Aristotle, who argued that it is solely the intellect that is immortal. Maimonides introduced the idea to Jewish philosophy. While he was careful because he didn't want to contradict the notion of the resurrection of the body, Maimonides, often in veiled, deliberately obscure language nonetheless believed that it is the mind that is immortal. If Maimonides were living now, he might take note of the fact that there is not necessarily a contradiction between an afterlife in God's Mind and bodily resurrection. To say that an afterlife existence implies only the option of immortality would be to limit God's options. It may be possible, for example, that the human mind will, after bodily death, reside for some time in God's Mind and at a later time that Mind will be reunited with its earthly body and be resurrected. The idea of an afterlife in God's Mind does not require the belief in bodily resurrection, but neither is bodily resurrection contradicted by that idea.

Supporters of Maimonides including Gersonides more vigorously supported the idea of the soul's immortality. And some aspect of the idea can be seen in Spinoza's thought.

The idea of a human mind existing after death in the Mind of God has two distinctively different possibilities. There is an immortality in which the mind lives on simply as memories in God's Mind or an immortality in which the human mind has an existing reality of its own in God's Mind.

It is more coherent with Judaism to believe the latter. A central premise of Judaism is that there is one, unified God, with a moral personality and a moral will, with a principal concern that humans behave morally. The goal of life, on this reading of Judaism, is for humans to acquire moral knowledge and act morally.

Therefore the idea of an afterlife in the Mind of God cannot, on moral grounds, be simply a Godly memory of the human's earthly existence. Such a static notion of an afterlife doesn't allow eternal compensation for earthly suffering or divine justice, reward or punishment based on the person's moral life on Earth. A dynamic afterlife suggests a continuing personal mind that allows for both compensation and justice.

Additionally, a continuing reality for the human mind in God's Mind allows for development for those with limited earthly opportunities for mental activities, such as those who died before birth, as infants, or at a young age and people with intellectual limitations. Some in this group have acquired fewer sense impressions, less knowledge, and have had fewer chances to make moral choices than people with a fully developed adult mind who have had the experience of acquiring knowledge and making moral choices. A continuing mind in the afterlife allows for this group to have a potential that is ongoing. That is, the mind's afterlife in the Mind of God is not dependent on acquired knowledge during a lifetime. One side effect of this view is that it makes all life equally precious.

One potential problem with this conception of a mental afterlife is that a focus on the mind that exists in the afterlife detracts from an appropriate focus on human activities. If, after all, we continue to exist in the Mind of God freed from physical limitations (e.g. pain, hunger, disease), then isn't there a chance that all our earthly hope and attention will be focused on the afterlife instead of on earthly life? In a sense, this question becomes: Is earthly existence independently important or it is just a prelude to the afterlife? Clearly, because we have it, it has to be of significant importance.

The Jewish revolution in history was to introduce the world to the idea of a moral God who needs human partners to act in the material world. The Jewish religious consciousness perceived that the Jewish people's relationship with God was one of human moral will in companionship with God's. The visionary insight of such an apprehension of the divine was that in pursuit of such moral companionship humans would elevate their own moral personalities.

This worldview profoundly affects the idea of an afterlife. Jews, for example, have moral tasks that are supposed to be performed in life, tasks both peculiar to the individual and to the individual's membership in the Jewish people and as part of humanity. Searching for these tasks is part of the human mission on Earth. The search, done through personal and communal revelations from God, leads to an understanding of moral tasks, undertaking the training to perform them, and then doing them. Within Judaism, these tasks might, for example, include: (1) encountering God and having a relationship with God; (2) marrying and raising a family; (3) studying Judaism; (4) engaging in lifelong learning about the world, its history, and the people in it as well as the nature of ethics and moral conduct; (5) supporting Israel and the Jewish people politically, financially, and in other ways; (6) having a moral occupation; and (7) developing skills to help with all the tasks.

One of these moral tasks is that we prepare as best we can for an eternal existence as a mind in the Mind of God. Because in the afterlife we will be judged, rewarded or punished, and we will be compensated for suffering on Earth, it is crucial to have a sense of justice. Because in the afterlife we may learn secrets about life on Earth that we didn't know, the more we know about the world the more we will be able to appreciate these secrets. Beyond that, the realm of the afterlife cannot be understood, but in some way memories of the earthly experience must be important. Since all the memories will reside in the surviving mind, accumulated experiences are important to have had on Earth.

But not all earthly knowledge acquired from thought and experience is equal. Therefore in preparation for the afterlife, humans can try to sift out the important knowledge from the trivial. It is much easier to consider what knowledge is important to fulfill our moral tasks on Earth than to determine knowledge that is important for eternity. Contentment after death relies on having completed the moral tasks we were supposed to fulfill on Earth and, perhaps, on the amount and nature of the knowledge we were able to acquire while living. Whatever experience we have in the afterlife, knowledge acquired on Earth should make the memories in the afterlife fuller and make it easier to acquire whatever new knowledge we get. That is one argument against suicide. It is an argument for old age. It provides an agenda for retirement: continue to acquire the knowledge one has not yet gathered in life. There can be a focus on literature to collect stories, philosophy to gain new insights about how we think about the world, art to contemplate beauty, the natural sciences and mathematics to understand the world, and the social sciences to understand the collective human endeavor.

It is crucial not just to acquire facts and interpretation of human existence but also a profound knowledge of ethics, including appropriate moral actions.

Is there a body of acquired knowledge about ethical questions that merits human study? One Jewish view is that such knowledge resides exclusively in the collected holy writings of Judaism. A more expansive, modern view includes encounters with God and the Jewish tradition but also includes a more comprehensive approach. Moral knowledge might be gained through the study of Jewish history as well as Jewish holy texts. Its emotional dimensions can be usefully grasped by the experience of mentally acquiring stories, such as by reading novels. Great novels can deal with moral complexities and ambiguities in a sophisticated way not always found in religious or ethical texts or studies. Characters in novels can act in ways people in real life can't. Readers can grasp the emotions these characters go through, the choices they have, the people they confront.

There are other questions about the idea of an afterlife in the Mind of God. Like the very idea of the afterlife, no one can know the answers to these questions. In some cases, only provisional answers can be attempted.

One question is about the mechanism of transformation at death from our minds to the Mind of God. Since God has access to all our thoughts throughout our lives, God has been accumulating our minds all along and finishes the process at our death so that our mind exists in the afterlife. But if that is so, then do our minds that currently exist in God's Mind while we are still alive continue to develop? It seems more likely that they remain static in God's Mind until our death when all the mental acts are collected in the mind and rendered active by God.

If the afterlife has no sensual delights, then should we prepare ourselves through a life on Earth full of sensory deprivations? There would be an argument for doing so if we could in any genuine sense replicate the realm of the afterlife on Earth. But we can't. All we do is expand our minds for use in the afterlife. There is therefore no useful argument for sensory deprivation.

What would it be like for the human mind in God's Mind? We would in some sense be in communion with God, but what would that be like? This is the part that remains the truest mystery. And there are ancillary elements to this mystery. Do we encounter other human minds such as our relatives, the people we treated well or mistreated, the famous we always wished to meet? Do we get answers to all the mysteries of life once we are in God's Mind? Can human minds in God's Mind receive prayers from people on Earth and give revelations like God? Do we continue to develop our minds in the afterlife, and, if so, how does the human mind continue to acquire knowledge in God's Mind? If we acquire all knowledge does the human mind become God-like?

It is impossible to understand the nature of the mind's afterlife in the Mind of God. The mind, after all, is in such a different realm in God's Mind than it is on Earth. It is a realm not like ours and beyond comprehension. In that realm we will have no sensations, and so our minds will be completely different from our earthly minds. If the human mind in God's Mind were like ours, it might be completely intolerable, because we'd be able to have thought but not act on it. It would be a sort of paralysis. That's partly why it is so difficult for humans to comprehend God. God, in another realm of human afterlife, does not act in this world other than by revelation, which is only a form of action. We get angry when God doesn't prevent an event or disaster because we would do so. But in the realms beyond life, there is no action that can be undertaken.

All that can finally be said about this realm is that we can't understand it on Earth, but we can prepare in some way by maintaining a relationship with God and acquiring knowledge, especially knowledge about justice and morality.

EXERCISES

Write an ethical will for any current or future children and grandchildren. The purpose of an ethical will is to transmit your values and your accumulated wisdom to your loved ones. Some ideas for an ethical will include:

1. As complete a family genealogy as you can create. This includes a history of each family member with names, birth and death dates, and locations and especially anecdotes about people.
2. A statement of what you believe to be true and guidelines for a good life and right behavior. This includes the lessons you have gleaned from life drawn both from right choices and wrong ones.
3. Apologies and requests for forgiveness for any bad moral actions.

Ethical wills can be brief or as extensive as a spiritual autobiography, a full memoir of your life including an explanation and rationale of your choices and decisions. An ethical will is the place to express what previously remained unexpressed. This can, for example, include a statement of love and devotion.

A Jewish ethical will is your statement of the basic beliefs of Judaism.

Which people that you have met deserve to be remembered and why? Make a list of those you either knew or have learned about who deserve to be recalled with honor and those who deserve not to be remembered.

A book about Jewish beliefs ought not end in death, but instead see the reality of death as a prompt to embrace life more forcefully than ever, to rededicate ourselves to improving our lives and the lives of as many other people as we can, and to remember that, in partnership with God, our lives have the highest meaning and, lived well, can do the greatest good.

GLOSSARY

Aggadah—The nonlegal Jewish writings such as ethics, theology, and folklore.

aliyah—To ascend or go up, *aliyah* means to go up to the bimah in a synagogue (the raised platform usually at the front) to say the required blessings before and after a Torah portion is read. *Aliyah* also means to immigrate to Israel.

Amidah—Also known as the Shemoneh Esrei or Tefillah, the Amidah refers to the nineteen prayers that make up a main part of the Jewish prayer service.

Ashkenazi—(pl. *Ashkenazim*) The Jews of central Europe who by tradition trace their ancestry to medieval Germany. There were major migrations to Poland and Russia between the twelfth and sixteenth centuries.

bar/bat mitzvah—The ceremonies at which young men (age thirteen) and young women (age twelve) come of age. More traditionally, they accept the obligation to obey the mitzvot that they are required to perform.

BCE—Before the Common Era, the religiously neutral designation meant to replace BC ("Before Christ").

bet din—A Jewish court of law.

Bible—The Hebrew Scriptures, the sacred writing of the Jewish people. Its first five books (Genesis, Exodus, Leviticus, Numbers, and Deuteronomy) are called the Torah. Christians call the Jewish Bible the Old Testament to indicate it was superseded by the New Testament. For the same reason, Jews do not generally use the term *Old Testament*.

bikkur cholim—Visiting and taking care of the sick.

CE—The Common Era, the religiously neutral designation meant to replace AD (Anno Domini, In the Year of Our Lord).

chesed—Showing kindness.

chuppah—A marriage canopy.

chutzpah—Yiddish for having an abundance of nerve and displaying it.

Conservative Judaism—One of the branches of Judaism. Conservative Judaism believes in the obligation to obey Jewish law and that the Halakhah evolves according to new insights and knowledge.

Diaspora—The dispersion of the Jewish people outside Palestine after the Babylonian exile or those living outside modern Israel.

Gemara—Completion of, or commentaries on, the Mishnah.

ger—A stranger, but by the Talmud the term referred to those who had become Jewish.

get—A bill of divorce.

Goy (plural *Goyim*)—A Gentile. The term itself is neutral, but it has taken on a derogatory connotation.

Halakhah—Jewish law.

Hasidism—A Jewish spiritual movement that began in the eighteenth century.

Kaddish—A prayer associated with mourning.

kashrut—The laws associated with keeping kosher, eating food according to Jewish law.

mensch—Yiddish for a genuine man, one who is mature, who helps others, who performs kindly deeds.

Midrash—An interpretation of a biblical verse.

minyan—The ten people (in tradition, men) required for a prayer service.

Mishnah—The code of Jewish law completed in 200 CE by Judah Ha-Nasi. The Mishnah plus the Gemara constitute the Talmud.

mitzvah—A Jewish ritual obligation. Also used, in a looser meaning, to refer to a good deed.

Orthodox Judaism—A branch of Judaism that considers Jewish law as binding.

rabbi—A trained Jewish interpreter of Jewish law, texts, and customs.

Reform Judaism—A Jewish movement that does not accept Jewish law as binding and seeks to fit Judaism within modernity.

Sephardim—Jews descended from those Jewish people who lived in Spanish countries.

Shabbat—The Sabbath.

Shema—A prayer emphasizing the unity of God.

Shoah—Genocide—refers to the murder of six million Jews during the Holocaust.

synagogue—A Jewish house of worship, also a shul and, in the Reform movement, sometimes a temple.

Torah—The first five books of the Bible. Also, the whole of Jewish wisdom.

tzedakah—Giving to charity.

BIBLIOGRAPHY

Adler, Rachel. *Engendering Judaism*. Philadelphia: Jewish Publication Society, 1998.

Agus, Jacob. *Guideposts in Modern Judaism: An Analysis of Current Trends in Jewish Thought*. New York: Bloch, 1954.

———. *The Jewish Quest: Essays on Basic Concepts of Jewish Theology*. New York: KTAV, 1983.

———. *Modern Philosophies of Judaism*. New York: Behrman, 1941.

Ariel, David S. *What Do Jews Believe?* New York: Schocken, 1995.

Ausubel, Nathan, ed. *A Treasury of Jewish Folklore*. New York: Bantam, 1980.

Baeck, Leo. *The Essence of Judaism*. New York: Schocken, 1961.

Bamberger, Bernard. *The Search for Jewish Theology*. New York: Behrman House, 1978.

Baron, Joseph L., ed. *A Treasury of Jewish Quotations*. New York: Crown, 1956.

Batnitzky, Leora. *How Judaism Became a Religion: An Introduction to Modern Jewish Thought*. Princeton, NJ: Princeton University Press, 2011.

Bellah, Robert N. *Religion in Human Evolution: From the Paleolithic to the Axial Age.* Cambridge, MA: Belknap Press of Harvard University Press, 2011.

Berger, Peter. *The Sacred Canopy.* Garden City, NY: Doubleday, 1969.

Berk, Sally Ann, ed. *The Big Little Book of Jewish Wit and Wisdom.* New York: Black Dog and Leventhal, 2000.

Berkovits, Eliezer. *Faith after the Holocaust.* New York: KTAV, 1973.

———. *God, Man and History.* Middle Village, NY: Jonathan David, 1959.

———. *Major Themes in Modern Philosophies of Judaism.* New York: KTAV, 1974.

Birnbaum, Philip. *Encyclopedia of Jewish Concepts.* New York: Hebrew Publishing Company, 1988.

Blech, Rabbi Benjamin. *The Complete Idiot's Guide to Understanding Judaism.* 2nd ed. New York: Alpha Books, 2003.

Borowitz, Eugene. *Choices in Modern Jewish Thought: A Partisan's Guide.* Springfield, NJ: Behrman, 1983.

———, ed. *Ehad: The Many Meanings of God Is One.* New York: Sh'ma, 1988.

———. *A New Jewish Theology in the Making.* Philadelphia: Westminster Press, 1968.

Breuer, Rabbi Dr. Joseph. *The Jewish Marriage: Source of Sanctity.* New York: Feldheim, 1956.

Brody, Seymour. *Jewish Heroes and Heroines of America.* Hollywood, FL: Lifeline, 1996.

Bronner, Leila Leah. *Journey to Heaven: Exploring Jewish Views of the Afterlife.* Jerusalem: Urim, 2011.

Buber, Martin. *I and Thou.* Trans. Walter Kaufmann. New York: Charles Scribner's Sons, 1970.

———. *On Judaism.* Edited by Nahum N. Glatzer. New York: Schocken, 1967.

The Chafetz Chayim. *Ahavath Chesed.* New York: Feldheim, 1976.

———. *The Concise Book of Mitzvoth.* New York, Feldheim, 1990.

Clorfene, Chaim, and Yaakov Rogalsky. *The Path of the Righteous Gentile: An Introduction to the Seven Laws of the Children of Noah.* Southfield, MI: Targum, 1987.

Cohen, A. *Everyman's Talmud.* New York: Schocken. 1975.

Cohen, Arthur A. *The Natural and the Supernatural Jew.* London: Vallentine, Mitchell, 1967.

Cohen, Arthur A., and Paul Mendes-Flohr, eds. *Contemporary Jewish Religious Thought.* New York: Free Press, 1987.

Cohn-Sherbok, Dan, ed. *Divine Intervention and Miracles in Jewish Theology.* Lewiston, NY: Edwin Mellen Press, 1996.

———. *The Jewish Heritage.* Oxford: Basil Blackwell, 1988.

———, ed. *Problems in Contemporary Jewish Theology.* Lewiston, NY: Edwin Mellen Press, 1991.

Cohon, Samuel S. *Essays in Jewish Theology.* Cincinnati, OH: HUC Press, 1987.

———. *Jewish Theology.* Assen, The Netherlands: Van Gorcum, 1971.

Cosgrove, Elliot J., ed. *Jewish Theology in Our Time: A New Generation Explores the Foundations and Future of Jewish Belief.* Woodstock, VT: Jewish Lights, 2010.

Davies, Paul. *Cosmic Jackpot: Why Our Universe Is Just Right for Life.* Boston: Houghton Mifflin Harcourt, 2007.

de Lange, Nicholas. *Judaism.* Oxford: Oxford University Press, 1986.

Dorff, Elliot N. *Conservative Judaism: Our Ancestors to Our Descendants.* New York: United Synagogue Youth, 1985.

———. *Mitzvah Means Commandment.* Edited by Avram Kogen. New York: United Synagogue Youth, 1989.

Dorff, Elliot N., and Louis E. Newman, eds. *Contemporary Jewish Theology: A Reader.* New York: Oxford University Press, 1999.

Editors of *Commentary* Magazine. *The Condition of Jewish Belief.* Northvale, NJ: Jason Aronson, 1989.

Eisen, Arnold M. *The Chosen People in America: A Study in Jewish Religious Ideology.* Bloomington: Indiana University Press, 1983.

Eisenstein, Ira, ed. *Varieties of Jewish Belief.* New York: Reconstructionist Press, 1966.

Elkins, Rabbi Dov Peretz, ed. *Jewish Stories from Heaven and Earth.* Woodstock, VT: Jewish Lights, 2008.

Ellenson, David. "An Insider View: A Defense of Theological Imprecision." *Judaism* 53, nos. 3–4 (Summer/Fall 2004): 176–81.

Ellenson, David, and Daniel Gordis. *Pledges of Jewish Allegiance: Conversion, Law, and Policymaking in Nineteenth- and Twentieth-Century Orthodox Responsa.* Stanford, CA: Stanford University Press, 2012.

Emet Ve-Emunah: Statement of Principles of Conservative Judaism. New York: Jewish Theological Seminary, Rabbinical Assembly, and United Synagogue, 1988.

Encyclopedia Judaica. 16 vols. Jerusalem: Keter, 1972.

Epstein, Isidore. *Judaism.* New York: Penguin, 1970.

Epstein, Lawrence J. *The Theory and Practice of Welcoming Converts to Judaism: Jewish Universalism.* Lewiston, ME: Edwin Mellen, 1992.

———. *A Treasury of Jewish Anecdotes.* Northvale, NJ: Jason Aronson, 1989.

———. *A Treasury of Jewish Inspirational Stories.* Northvale, NJ: Jason Aronson, 1993.

Fackenheim, Emil. "Can We Believe in Judaism Religiously?" *Commentary* 6 (December 1948): 521–27.

———. *God's Presence in History.* New York: Harper, 1970.

———. *A Quest for Past and Future: Essays in Jewish Theology.* Boston: Beacon Press, 1968.

———. *To Mend the World: Foundations of Post-Holocaust Jewish Thought.* Bloomington: Indiana University Press, 1994.

Falcon, Rabbi Ted, and David Blatner. *Judaism for Dummies.* Hoboken, NJ: Wiley, 2001

Fishbane, Michael. *Sacred Attunement: A Jewish Theology.* Chicago: University of Chicago Press, 2008.

Fowler, James W. *Stages of Faith.* New York: Harper & Row, 1981.

Friedlander, Albert H. *Leo Baeck.* Woodstock, NY: Overlook Press, 1991.

Friedlander, M. *The Jewish Religion.* 6th ed. London: Shapiro, Vallentine and Co., 1935.

Friedman, Maurice S. *Martin Buber: The Life of Dialogue.* Chicago: University of Chicago Press, 1955.

Friedman, Richard Elliot. *Who Wrote the Bible?* New York: Summit Books, 1987.

Gastwirth, Paul. "Concepts of God." *Religious Studies* 8, no. 2 (1972): 147–52.

Gillman, Neil. *The Death of Death: Resurrection and Immortality in Jewish Thought.* Woodstock, VT: Jewish Lights, 1997.

———. *Doing Jewish Theology: God, Torah and Israel in Modern Judaism.* Woodstock, VT: Jewish Lights, 2008.

———. *Sacred Fragments: Recovering Theology for the Modern Jew.* Philadelphia: Jewish Publication Society, 1990.

———. *The Way into Encountering God in Judaism.* Woodstock, VT: Jewish Lights, 2000.

Glatzer, Nahum N., ed. *Franz Rosenzweig: His Life and Thought.* Philadelphia: Jewish Publication Society, 1953.

———. *Modern Jewish Thought: A Source Reader.* New York: Schocken, 1977.

Goldberg, David J., and John D. Rayner. *The Jewish People: Their History and Their Religion.* New York: Viking, 1987.

Goldy, Robert G. *The Emergence of Jewish Theology in America.* Bloomington: Indiana University Press, 1990.

Gordis, Robert. *Conservative Judaism: An American Philosophy.* New York: Behrman House, 1945.

———. *A Faith for Moderns.* New York: Bloch, 1960.

Graupe, Heinz Mosche. *The Systematic Nature of Jewish Theology: Two Examples.* Chicago: Academy Chicago Publishers, 1995.

Green, Arthur. *Seek My Face, Speak My Name: A Contemporary Jewish Theology.* Northvale, NJ: Jason Aronson, 1992.

Greenberg, Hayiim. "The Universalism of the Chosen People." *The Inner Eye* 1 (1953).

Greenberg, Simon. *Foundations of a Faith.* New York: Burning Bush Press, 1967.

Gross, David C. *Dictionary of 1,000 Jewish Proverbs.* New York: Hippocrene, 1997.

Guttman, Julius. *Philosophies of Judaism.* Translated by David W. Silverman. New York: Schocken, 1976.

Haberman, Joshua. "Salomon Ludwig Steinheim's Doctrine of Revelation." *Judaism* 17 (1968).

Halberstam, Yitta, and Judith Leventhal. *Small Miracles for the Jewish Heart*. Avon, MA: Adams, 2002.

Halivni, David Weiss. *Breaking the Tablets: Jewish Theology After the Shoah*. Lanham, MD: Rowman & Littlefield, 2007.

Halpern, Salomon Alter. *Tales of Faith*. 2nd ed. New York: Feldheim, 1972.

Harris, Sam. *Free Will*. New York: Free Press, 2012.

Hartman, David. *The God Who Hates Lies: Confronting and Rethinking Jewish Tradition*. Woodstock, VT: Jewish Lights, 2011.

Herberg, Will. *Judaism and Modern Man*. New York: Farrar, Straus and Young, 1951.

Hertzberg, Arthur, ed. *Judaism*. New York: George Braziller, 1962.

Heschel, Abraham Joshua. *God in Search of Man*. Philadelphia: Jewish Publication Society, 1956.

———. *Man Is Not Alone*. New York: Farrar, Straus and Giroux, 1951.

———. *Man's Quest for God*. New York: Scribner, 1954.

———. *The Prophets*. Philadelphia: Jewish Publication Society, 1962.

Hick, John H. *Philosophy of Religion*. 4th ed.. Englewood Cliffs, NJ: Prentice-Hall, 1990.

Himmelfarb, Milton. "What Do American Jews Believe?" *Commentary* 102, no. 2 (August 1996): 18–96.

Holtz, Barry W., ed. *Back to the Sources: Reading the Classic Jewish Texts*. New York: Summit, 1984.

———. *The Schocken Guide to Jewish Books*. New York: Schocken, 1992.

Hudson, Yeager. *The Philosophy of Religion*. Mountain View, CA: Mayfield, 1991.

Husik, Isaac. *A History of Mediaeval Jewish Philosophy*. New York: Atheneum, 1974.

Jacobs, Louis. *The Book of Jewish Belief*. New York: Behrman House, 1984.

———. *The Book of Jewish Practice*. West Orange, NJ: Behrman House, 1987.

———. *Faith*. London: Vallentine, Mitchell, 1968.

———. *The Jewish Religion: A Companion*. New York: Oxford University Press, 1995.

———. *A Jewish Theology*. New York: Behrman House, 1973.

———. *Jewish Thought Today*. New York: Behrman House, 1970.

———. *Judaism and Theology: Essays on the Jewish Religion*. London: Vallentine, Mitchell, 2005.

———. *Principles of the Jewish Faith*. New York: Commentary Classic, 1964.

———. *Theology in the Responsa*. London: Routledge and Kegan Paul, 1975.

———. *A Tree of Life: Diversity, Flexibility, and Creativity in Jewish Law*. Oxford: Oxford University Press, 1984.

———. *We Have Reason to Believe: Some Aspects of Jewish Theology Examined in the Light of Modern Thought*. London: Vallentine Mitchell, 2004.

The Jewish Encyclopedia. 12 vols. New York: Funk and Wagnalls, 1901.

Joseph, Morris. *Judaism as Creed and Life*. New York: Macmillan, 1903.

Kaplan, Mordecai. *Judaism as a Civilization*. New York: Schocken, 1972.

———. *The Meaning of God in Modern Jewish Religion*. The Jewish Reconstructionist Foundation, 1947.

Katz, Steven T., ed. *The Impact of the Holocaust on Jewish Theology*. New York: NYU Press, 2007.

———. *Jewish Philosophers*. New York: Bloch, 1975.

Kaufmann, Yehezkel. *The Religion of Israel: From Its Beginnings to the Babylonian Exile*. Translated by Moshe Greenberg. Chicago: University of Chicago Press, 1960.

Kellner, Menachem. *Dogma in Medieval Jewish Thought*. New York: Oxford, 1986.

———. *Must a Jew Believe Anything?* 2nd ed. Portland, OR: Littman Library of Jewish Civilization, 2006

Kepnes, Steven D. "A Narrative Jewish Theology." *Judaism* 37, no. 2 (Spring 1988): 210–17.

Kessler, Edward. *What Do Jews Believe? The Customs and Culture of Modern Judaism*. New York: Walker, 2007.

Kieval, Herman. *The Theology of Judaism as Reflected in the Prayerbook*. New York: Torah Institute, 1975.

Kirsch, Jonathan. *God Against the Gods: The History of the War between Monotheism and Polytheism.* New York: Penguin, 1964.

Klein, Judith Weinstein. *Jewish Identity and Self-Esteem.* New York: American Jewish Committee, 1980.

Kohler, Kaufmann. *Jewish Theology Systematically and Historically Considered.* New York: Macmillan, 1928.

Kristol, Irving. "How Basic Is Basic Judaism?" *Commentary* 5 (January 1948): 27–34.

Kurzweil, Arthur. *Kabbalah for Dummies.* Hoboken, NJ: Wiley, 2007.

Kushner, Harold. *When Bad Things Happen to Good People.* New York: Schocken, 1981.

———. "Why Do the Righteous Suffer? Notes towards a Theology of Tragedy." *Judaism* 28, no. 3 (Summer 1979): 316–23.

Levenson, Jon D. *Creation and the Persistence of Evil: The Jewish Drama of Divine Omnipotence.* Princeton, NJ: Princeton University Press, 1994.

Levy, Hans, Alexander Altmann, and Isaak Heineman, eds. *Three Jewish Philosophers.* New York: Atheneum, 1973.

Levy, Solomon. *Jewish Theology.* London: Williams, Lea & Co., 1920.

Lichtenstein, Aaron. *The Seven Laws of Noah.* 2nd ed. New York: Rabbi Jacob Joseph School Press, 1986.

Lubarsky, Sandra B., and David Ray Griffin. *Jewish Theology and Process Thought.* Albany: State University of New York Press, 1996.

Luhrmann, T. M. *When God Talks Back: Understanding the American Evangelical Relationship with God.* New York: Knopf, 2012.

Luzzatto, Moshe Chayim. *The Path of the Just.* New York: Feldheim, 1966.

———. *The Way of God.* New York: Feldheim, 1977.

Maimonides, Moses. *The Guide for the Perplexed.* New York: Dover, 1956.

Martin, Bernard. *Contemporary Reform Jewish Thought.* Chicago: Central Conference of American Rabbis, 1968.

McGrath, Alister. *A Fine-Tuned Universe: The Quest for God in Science and Theology.* Louisville, KY: Westminster John Knox Press, 2009.

Meyer, Michael A. *Response to Modernity: A History of the Reform Movement in Judaism.* Detroit: Wayne State University Press, 1988.

Montefiore, C. G., and H. M. J. Loewe. *A Rabbinic Anthology.* New York: Schocken, 1974.

Nelson, Rabbi David W. *Judaism, Physics and God.* Woodstock, VT: Jewish Lights, 2006.

Neusner, Jacob. *Judaism States Its Theology: The Talmudic Re-Presentation.* Atlanta, GA: Scholars Press, 1993.

———. *Judaism's Theological Voice: The Melody of the Talmud.* Chicago: University of Chicago Press, 1995.

———. *The Theological Foundations of Rabbinic Midrash.* Lanham, MD: University Press of America, 2006.

———. *The Theology of the Oral Torah.* Montreal: McGill-Queen's University Press, 1999.

———. *Understanding Jewish Theology: Classical Issues and Modern Perspectives.* New York: KTAV, 1973.

Newman, Louis E. *An Introduction to Jewish Ethics.* Upper Saddle River, NJ: Pearson, 2005.

Noveck, Simon. *Milton Steinberg: Portrait of a Rabbi.* New York: KTAV, 1978.

Och, Bernard. "Creation and Redemption: Towards a Theology of Creation." *Judaism* 44, no. 2 (Spring 1995): 226–43.

Olitzky, Rabbi Kerry M. *Introducing My Faith and My Community: The Jewish Outreach Institute Guide for the Christian in a Jewish Interfaith Relationship.* Woodstock, VT: Jewish Lights, 2004.

Parzen, Herbert. *Architects of Conservative Judaism.* New York: Jonathan David, 1964.

Perlman, Lawrence. *Abraham Heschel's Idea of Revelation.* Atlanta, GA: Scholars Press, 1989.

Petuchowski, Jakob. "The Question of Jewish Theology." *Judaism* 7 (Winter 1958): 49–55.

Plaut, W. Gunther. *Book of Proverbs: A Commentary.* New York: UAHC, 1961.

———. *The Torah: A Modern Commentary.* New York: Union of American Hebrew Congregations, 1981.

Pogrebin, Abigail. *Stars of David: Prominent Jews Talk about Being Jewish.* New York: Broadway Books, 2005.

Prager, Dennis. *A Brief Introduction to Ethical Monotheism.* DVD.

Prager, Dennis, and Joseph Telushkin. *The Nine Questions People Ask About Judaism.* New York: Simon and Schuster, 1981.

———. *Why the Jews? The Reason for Antisemitism.* New York: Touchstone, 2003.

Raphael, Simcha Paull. *Jewish Views of the Afterlife.* Northvale, NJ: Jason Aronson, 1994.

Ratner, Joseph. *The Philosophy of Spinoza.* New York: Modern Library, 1954.

Reimer, Jack, and Nathaniel Stampfer, eds. *So That Your Values Live On—Ethical Wills and How to Prepare Them.* Woodstock, VT: Jewish Lights, 1991.

Robinson, George. *Essential Judaism: A Complete Guide to Beliefs, Customs, and Rituals.* New York: Pocket Books, 2000.

Rosenzweig, Franz. *On Jewish Learning.* New York: Schocken, 1955.

———. *The Star of Redemption.* Boston: Beacon, 1971.

Rosten, Leo. *Leo Rosten's Treasury of Jewish Quotations.* New York: Bantam, 1980.

Roth, Leon. *Judaism: A Portrait.* New York: Viking, 1961.

Sachar, Howard M. *The Course of Modern Jewish History.* Revised edition. New York: Vintage, 1990.

Schechter, Solomon. *Aspects of Rabbinic Theology.* New York: Schocken, 1961.

———. *The Dogmas of Judaism.* Studies in Judaism. New York: Atheneum, 1970.

Scholem, Gershom. *Major Trends in Jewish Mysticism.* New York: Schocken, 1941.

Schroeder, Gerald L. *Genesis and the Big Bang.* New York: Bantam, 1990.

Schulweis, Harold M. *For Those Who Can't Believe.* New York: Harper-Collins, 1994.

———. "Theological Modesty and the Idea of Divine Perfection." *Judaism* 25, no. 4 (Fall 1976): 489–93.

Schwartz, Barry L. *Jewish Theology: A Comparative Study*. West Orange, NJ: Behrman House, 1991.

Schwarz, Leo W., ed. *Great Ages and Ideas of the Jewish People*. New York: Modern Library, 1956.

Seeskin, Kenneth. "Evil and the Morality of God" (book review). *Judaism* 35, no. 1 (Winter 1986): 117–19.

———. *Jewish Philosophy in a Secular Age*. Albany: State University of New York Press, March 1990.

———. "The Perfection of God and the Presence of Evil." *Judaism* 31, no. 2 (Spring 1982): 202–10.

———. "The Reality of Radical Evil." *Judaism* 29, no. 4 (Fall 1980): 440–53.

Seltzer, Robert M. *Jewish People, Jewish Thought: The Jewish Experience in History*. New York: Macmillan, 1980.

Sherwin, Byron L. *Faith Finding Meaning: A Theology of Judaism*. Oxford: Oxford University Press, 2009.

———. *Toward a Jewish Theology*. Lewiston, ME: Edwin Mellen Press, 1991.

Soloveitchik, Joseph B. *The Lonely Man of Faith*. New York: Doubleday, 2006.

Sonsino, Rifat, and Daniel B. Syme. *Finding God: Ten Jewish Responses*. Rev. ed. New York: URJ Press, 2002.

———. *What Happens After I Die: Jewish Views of Life After Death*. New York: UAHC Press, 1990.

Steinberg, Milton. *Anatomy of Faith*. Edited by Arthur A. Cohen. New York: Harcourt, Brace, 1960.

———. *Basic Judaism*. New York: Harcourt, Brace & World, 1947.

Steinsaltz, Adin. *The Essential Talmud*. New York: Bantam, 1977.

———. *The Thirteen Petalled Rose: A Discourse on the Essence of Jewish Existence and Belief*. New York: Basic Books, 2006.

Tanakh. Philadelphia: Jewish Publication Society, 1985.

Telushkin, Rabbi Joseph. *A Code of Jewish Ethics*. Vol. 1: *You Shall Be Holy*. New York: Bell Tower, 2006.

———. *A Code of Jewish Ethics*. Vol. 2: *Love Your Neighbor as Yourself*. New York: Bell Tower, 2009.

———. *Jewish Literacy.* New York: Morrow, 1991.

———. *Jewish Wisdom.* New York: Morrow, 1994.

Troster, Lawrence. "Asymmetry, Negative Entropy and the Problem of Evil." *Judaism* 34, no 4 (Fall 1985): 453–61.

Vial, Theodore M., and Mark A. Hadley. *Ethical Monotheism, Past and Present.* Providence, RI: Brown Judaica Studies, 2001.

Vogel, Manfred H. *A Quest for a Theology of Judaism.* Lanham, MD: University Press of America, 1987.

Wein, Rabbi Beryl. *Basic Beliefs of Judaism: What It Means to Be Jewish* (audio cassette). The Destiny Foundation, 2005.

Weiss-Rosmarin, Trude. *Judaism and Christianity: The Differences.* New York: Jonathan David, 1943.

Wiesenthal, Simon. *The Sunflower.* New York: Schocken, 1998.

Wigoder, Geoffrey. *The Encyclopedia of Judaism.* New York: Macmillan, 1989.

Wolpe, David J. "The Human Implications of Revelation." *Judaism* 36, no. 3 (Summer 1987): 278–82.

———. *Why Be Jewish?* New York: Holt, 1995.

———. *Why Faith Matters.* New York: HarperOne, 2009.

Wyschogrod, Michael. *The Body of Faith.* Minneapolis, MN: Seabury, 1983.

WEBSITES

American Jewish Archives, americanjewisharchives.org
Central Conference of American Rabbis (Reform), ccarnet.org
Clal, clal.org
Hazon, hazon.org
IKAR, ikar-la.org
Jerusalem Post, jpost.com
Jewish Ideas Daily, jewishideasdaily.com
Jewish Outreach Institute, joi.org
Jewish Reconstructionist Movement, jewishrecon.org
Jewish Telegraphic Agency, jta.org
Jewish Virtual Library, jewishvirtuallibrary.org

The Jewish Week, thejewishweek.com
Louis Jacobs, louisjacobs.org
Mazon: A Jewish Response to Hunger, mazon.org
Orthodox Union, ou.org
Rabbinical Assembly (Conservative), rabbinicalassembly.org
Tablet magazine, tabletmag.org
Times of Israel, timesofisrael.com
Union for Reform Judaism, urj.org
The United Synagogue of Conservative Judaism, uscj.org
Yad Vashem, yadvashem.org

INDEX